Complete Library Skills Activities Program

Ready-to-Use Lessons for Grades K–6

Arden Druce

Illustrated by Carol Ditter Waters

THE CENTER FOR APPLIED
RESEARCH IN EDUCATION
West Nyack, New York 10995

Library of Congress Cataloging-in-Publication Data

Druce, Arden.
    Complete library skills activities program.
    "An earlier edition of this work was published as
Library skills: lessons for grades K–6, by Dick
Whittington Press, 1986"—T.p. verso.
    ISBN 0-87628-240-0
    1. Elementary school libraries—Activity programs.
2. School children—Library orientation.   3. Kinder
garten—Activity programs.   I. Waters, Carol Ditter.
II. Title.
Z675.S3D79   1990   89-22342
025.5′678′222   CIP

Printed in the United States of America

10   9   8   7

C2400-4

ISBN 0-87628-240-0

**THE CENTER FOR APPLIED RESEARCH
IN EDUCATION**
West Nyack, NY 10994
A Simon & Schuster Company

On the World Wide Web at http://www.phdirect.com

Prentice-Hall International (UK) Limited, *London*
Prentice-Hall of Australia Pty. Limited, *Sydney*
Prentice-Hall Canada Inc., *Toronto*
Prentice-Hall Hispanoamericana, S.A., *Mexico*
Prentice-Hall of India Private Limited, *New Delhi*
Prentice-Hall of Japan, Inc., *Tokyo*
Simon & Schuster Asia Pte. Ltd., *Singapore*
Editora Prentice-Hall do Brasil, Ltda., *Rio de Janeiro*

About the Author

During the twenty-one years Arden Druce served as a teacher and school librarian in elementary, junior, and senior high schools, she wrote, compiled, and taught library skills lessons. On the day before she retired in 1986, a fellow teacher remarked that there would be no one at the school to teach library skills any more. This chance remark inspired her to write this book.

On the elementary school level, in addition to library skills, the author specialized in storytelling, using her collection of ninety-eight flannel board stories (most of which she made herself) and seventy-five puppets.

She has had a number of her writings published, including seven paper-bag puppet books, no longer in print, and miscellaneous articles and book reviews.

Arden Druce now devotes her time to writing, studying, and animal welfare.

About This Resource

The *Complete Library Skills Activities Program: Ready-to-Use Lessons for Grades K–6* is a distillation of twenty-one years of library experience. The lesson plans, which include objectives, materials, preparation, and follow-up, tell you exactly what to say when presenting a lesson. Worksheets, for quick reproduction, are included. Answers are provided.

It is best to follow the lessons as they are presented, so that each new skill has the necessary foundation laid by preceding lessons. However, you should feel free to choose skills from any grade level, if the skills are appropriate for your students.

Lessons for kindergarten through second grade (Units K through 2) teach the basics of book care, library behavior, listening skills, and appreciating books. Lessons for third grade (Unit 3) teach students how to find their way through a book and understand its parts and their uses. The lessons for fourth through six grades (Units 4 through 6) begin with pretests (found in Appendix B) to determine at which skill level a class needs to begin. For example, if a sixth grade class has not studied title pages, it has no foundation upon which to learn the card catalog. The necessary vocabulary—fiction, nonfiction, author, title, illustrator, publisher, copyright, and so forth—may not have been mastered. Pretest results will indicate whether the class has a thorough foundation and can begin with Unit 6 or whether it needs to begin with Unit 3, 4, or 5.

How frequently a lesson is taught depends on you and your class. Some teachers choose to teach one lesson a week. Others decide to teach an entire unit and, therefore, may decide to teach one lesson a day for a limited period of time. However, the main determinant is probably the class. If a pretest indicates that a sixth grade class has not had previous library training, the directive titled "What to Teach in Sixth Grade" in the beginning of Unit 6 recommends starting with Unit 3. If you teach Units 3 through 6 in sequence, you will have to cover forty-eight lessons. The number of lessons you wish to teach, of course, determines the frequency of lessons.

COVERAGE

The Table of Contents outlines the basic coverage of this manual. A number of special features, such as the appendices "Books to Read Aloud," "Publish-a-Book Contest," and "Addresses of Authors, Illustrators, and Publishers," follow Unit 6.

Dictionary skills are beyond the scope of this manual and are thus not covered. Advanced skills appropriate for junior high, such as using reference books, bibliographies, the *Readers' Guide,* and so forth, have likewise not been included.

REPRODUCIBLE MATERIALS

Worksheets for you to reproduce are provided with the lessons for which they are designed. Answers to the worksheets are found in Appendix C. Reproducible pretests for grades 4, 5, and 6 are located in Appendix B. An answer key is included. Each answer is accompanied by a note indicating which lesson introduced the item.

LESSON PLANS

Each lesson plan includes objectives, materials, preparation, and follow-up. Each plan also tells you exactly what to say, which you may of course modify to suit your own needs. Questions asked in each lesson are followed by their answers in parentheses. Practice items for the chalkboard are also followed by their answers in parentheses. When copying the practice items, be careful not to copy the answers!

Arden Druce

Some Suggestions

1. If a specific book you need is not in your school library, you can obtain it through one of the following means: (a) Phone your local public library and ask the reference librarian if the library has the book. If so, ask if the book is in. If the library has the book, but it is not in, you will probably have to go to the library to fill out a request for it. However, if it is in, ask the librarian to hold it for you. Libraries will usually hold books a few days. (b) If your public library doesn't have the book, ask the librarian to obtain it through an interlibrary loan.

2. Always have several books on hand from which you can read aloud. If your class has heard a book, you can quickly pick up another. However, students often like to hear familiar stories. If a student says, "I've already heard that story," you can reply, "Well, then, you know it's a good story."

3. Teachers should provide alphabetizing practice every day. The lack of alphabetizing skills is one of the greatest obstacles to mastering library skills.

4. Alternate the method of checking worksheets. Sometimes check papers with the students. Other times check them yourself. Always return them.

5. Reinforce skills intermittently throughout the year when needed.

6. Students need a great amount of drill; so drill, drill, drill.

7. Before you teach a lesson, have the students put their pencils away.

8. If you have a library, point out where the various sections are located as you cover them in the lessons, for example, picture books, easy books, fiction, nonfiction, and reference books.

9. Adhere to the rule that students are always to read silently before reading aloud. This rule applies to reading chalkboard material, too. It isn't appropriate to ask a student to read aloud from the board until he or she has had time to read the material silently first.

10. Examples of title pages, tables of contents, catalog cards, and so forth may be put on the board or used on an overhead projector instead of being dittoed. These alternatives save paper, sidestep broken duplicators, and provide a change of presentation.

11. Divide the class into groups (e.g., a boy group and a girl group) when doing active library lessons such as using the card catalog, locating specific books, and so forth. This makes it easier to see that each student participates.

12. When students are assigned to use card catalog guide cards, check each student to see if he or she is really using the guides.

13. Vitalize lesson presentations by alternating among different visual materials such as dittos, the chalkboard, and the flannel board.

14. Encourage your students to get a public library card and to use it.

15. First and second grade teachers may want to use the words *author, title,* and *illustrator* when they are reading aloud to their students.

16. You may want to schedule library periods for half an hour. This allows fifteen minutes, if needed, for the lesson and fifteen minutes for checking out books. Extra time would be needed and could be scheduled for some lessons such as practice using the card catalog.

17. Excuse students to line up for recess by asking questions based on their library lessons. For example, ask, "What is an author?"

18. Excuse tables of students in the library to line up by asking questions based on their library lessons. If a student gets the right answer, his or her whole table gets to line up.

19. Use a green (go) marker and a red (stop) marker to designate the lessons you are to teach your students.

Acknowledgments

For invaluable contributions, I am especially indebted to the following individuals and organizations:

Margo Fischer, third grade teacher, who gave so generously of her expertise and time in reading and suggesting ideas for this book

Carol Spears, first grade teacher, who so perceptively suggested ideas on listening

Bonnie Olson, second grade teacher, who graciously read and evaluated lessons from this book

Virginia Estrala, fifth grade teacher, who, in her appreciation of and desire to continue the lessons I taught her classes, inspired me to write this book

Carol Ditter Waters, artist–associate, who drew the book's delightful illustrations

Ramona Ragsdale, my mother, who lovingly gave me complete support in this endeavor

Janet T. Peterson, permissions editor of *The World Book Encyclopedia,* who was most gracious and generous in granting reprint rights

Karen L. Mabry, technical adviser, for her generous and valuable assistance

World Book, Inc., for granting permission to reprint from *The World Book Encyclopedia* material about Lapland, Log Cabin, Insect Study Aids, the Index, and Special Features

Gateway Press, Inc., for granting permission to reprint the index from *Colonial America*

Raintree Publishers, for information relating to the Publish-a-Book Contest

School Library Journal, for permission to reprint "A Story About the Dewey Decimal System of Classification"

American Library Association, for permission to reprint the "Booklist" review of *Star Boy*

Contents

PART 2: APPENDICES • 257

PART **1**

Library
Skills
Lessons

UNIT K

KINDERGARTEN

What to Teach in Kindergarten

SUGGESTIONS

1. Before your first trip to the library, refer to Appendix A, "How to Conduct Library Visits."
2. You may want to use a green (go) marker and a red (stop) marker to designate the pages you need to teach.

LESSONS

Teach Lessons 1 through 13.

Lesson 1. What a Library Is and How to Behave in One

OBJECTIVES

1. To teach what a library is
2. To discuss the need for quiet in the library
3. To read a book to the students

MATERIAL

The book *Quiet! There's a Canary in the Library* by Don Freeman (Childrens' Press, 1969). (If this book is not available, read another worthwhile book. For some suggestions, see Appendix D, "Books to Read Aloud.")

LESSON

If you have a school library, you may want to teach this lesson immediately before your first visit. (Some kindergarten teachers don't feel that their students are ready for library visitations until the latter part of the first semester.) However, if your students are visiting a public library on their own, this lesson may be needed now.

If you don't have a library, teach this lesson any time. However, if you teach it now, you will be able to progress through the lessons consecutively. Also, your students may be visiting a public library on their own, and this lesson will be of value to them.

Who knows what a library is?

If you need to add to or clarify students' definitions, refer to the following: A library is a room or building where there are many books for reading.

Have you ever been to a library?

We have (don't have) a library at our school.

There may be a public library near your home.

The person who takes care of a library is called a *librarian*. Sometimes school libraries don't have librarians; they have library clerks.

If your school has a librarian, tell the students the librarian's name. If your school has a library clerk instead of a librarian, or in addition to a librarian, tell the students the clerk's name.

Some people call a l*ibr*ary a l*iberry*. They should call it a l*ibr*ary. Let's say l*ibr*ary together: l*ibr*ary.

Can you buy the books in a library?

Can you read books in a library?

Can you check books out of a library?

If you check a book out of a library, you are responsible for it. You must not let the book get hurt or damaged. You must also take the book back on time.

How do you know when it's time to take a book back to the library?

Can you return your book before the date stamped inside?

People go to libraries to read or check books out.

We are always very quiet in libraries. We don't want to disturb anyone.

When we leave a library, we always put our chairs back just as we found them. We want to keep the library neat so everyone can enjoy it.

Inform the students that you are going to read a book to them.

Be very quiet and still while I'm reading.

If you aren't quiet, you won't be able to hear the story.

The other students won't be able to hear either.

It's courteous to be quiet when someone is reading or speaking to you.

Hold up the book, with pictures facing the students.

Listen.

Standing to the side of the book, read aloud in an interesting way.
Praise the students if they behaved well. If they didn't, discuss how they can improve their behavior.

SUGGESTIONS

1. Before your first library visit, refer to Appendix A, "How to Conduct Library Visits."
2. Consider how responsible your students are when deciding whether to let them take school library books home. Some kindergarten teachers let their students take books home after Christmas.

Lesson 2. How to Keep Books Clean

OBJECTIVES

1. To teach students to keep books clean
2. To read a book to the class

MATERIALS

1. A book that is soiled. If you don't have one, a clean book can be used.
2. A book to read aloud (For some suggestions, see Appendix D, "Books to Read Aloud.")

LESSON

Hold up the soiled or clean book for the class to see.

> Would you rather look at a book that is clean or a book that is dirty?
>
> How can we keep books clean?
>
> We should always have clean hands when we handle books.
>
> What would happen if we handled books when our hands were dirty?
>
> We should be careful when we lay a book down. We should make sure that the place where we are going to put the book is dry and clean. We don't lay books where there is paste or paint or anything else that would hurt them.

Inform the students that you are going to read a book to them.

Tell them that they should be quiet and still. If you need to, discuss the reasons: so they can hear, so the other students can hear, to be courteous to the person who is reading.

After the story, praise the students for being quiet and still and for listening, if praise is deserved. If the students didn't behave well, discuss how they can improve their behavior.

Lesson 3. How to Lay Down a Book

OBJECTIVES

1. To teach students to lay books down gently
2. To read a book to the class

MATERIAL

A book to read aloud. (For some suggestions, see Appendix D, "Books to Read Aloud.")

LESSON

> Books are our friends. We love them.
>
> We always handle them gently. We never slam them down. We lay them down carefully.

Demonstrate how to lay a book down gently.

> Who can show us how to lay a book down?

Choose some students, one at a time, to demonstrate.

Inform the students that you are going to read a book to them.

Tell them that they should be quiet and still. If you need to, discuss the reasons: so they can hear, so the other students can hear, to be courteous to the person who is reading.

Listen.

Read the book in an interesting way.

Praise the students for being quiet and still and for listening, if praise is deserved. If the students didn't behave well, discuss how they can improve their behavior.

Lesson 4. Books Aren't Toys

OBJECTIVES

1. To teach students that books aren't toys
2. To read a book to the class

MATERIAL

A book to read aloud. (For some suggestions, see Appendix D, "Books to Read Aloud.")

LESSON

Books aren't toys. We don't play with them; they are for reading.

We don't twirl them around on the desk or throw them to someone.

We handle them very gently.

Inform the students that you are going to read a book to them.

Tell them that they should be quiet and still. If you need to, discuss the reasons: so they can hear, so the other students can hear, to be courteous to the person who is reading.

Listen.

Read the book in an interesting way.

Praise the students for being quiet and still and for listening, if praise is deserved. If the students didn't behave well, discuss how they can improve their behavior.

Lesson 5. Why We Don't Write or Color in Books

OBJECTIVES

1. To teach students not to write or color in books
2. To read a book to the class

MATERIALS

1. A box of scratch paper (For demonstration purposes, place on top of the pile a piece of scratch paper that has been used on one side, a piece that has a corner torn off, and a piece of an unusual size.)
2. One or more books on which someone has written or colored (If a defaced book is not available, teach the lesson anyway.)
3. A book to read aloud (For some suggestions, see Appendix D, "Books to Read Aloud.")

LESSON

Hold up a piece of scratch paper.

> This is a piece of scratch paper. Scratch paper is paper that has been used on one side, that has been damaged, or that has an unusual size.

Show a piece of scratch paper that has been used on one side. Show another piece that has the corner torn off. Show a piece that is an unusual size.

> I'm going to keep a box of scratch paper here.

Designate the place.

> When you want to write or color, you may get some scratch paper. You don't need to ask for permission.

If possible, present one or more books in which someone has written or colored.

> Sometimes students write or color in books.

> Do you think they should do that?

> Do we like clean books or books that have been made ugly with writing and coloring?

> We never write or color on books.

If you want to write or color, you may get some scratch paper. You may write or color on scratch paper as much as you want. But you must never write or color in books.

Inform the students that you are going to read a book to them.

Tell them that they should be quiet and still. If you need to, discuss the reasons: so they can hear, so the other students can hear, to be courteous to the one sharing.

Listen.

Read the book in an interesting way.

Praise the students for being quiet and still and for listening, if praise is deserved. If the students weren't well behaved, discuss how they can improve.

SUGGESTION

Instead of presenting scratch paper as an alternative to writing in books, you may want to put out "special" drawing paper or even make up blank booklets for students to use. (Some teachers and librarians feel that scratch paper may not seem as "official" and appealing to students as drawing paper or blank booklets.)

Lesson 6. How to Carry a Book

OBJECTIVES

1. To teach students the proper way to carry books
2. To read a book to the class

MATERIAL

A book to read aloud. (For some suggestions, see Appendix D, "Books to Read Aloud.")

LESSON

When we are carrying books we need to be very careful so we don't drop them.

We never put them on our heads; they might fall and get hurt.

We carry books under our arms or against our bodies.

Demonstrate. Hold a book at your side and against your chest.

Who can show us how to hold a book?

Have one or more students demonstrate the proper ways to hold a book.

We never throw a book. We love books, and we treat them gently.

If you take good care of your books, you may be able to keep them for your whole life.

I've had some of my books since I was five or six years old. I'm going to keep them forever.

Inform the students that you are going to read a book to them.
Tell them that they should be quiet and still. If you need to, discuss the reasons: so they can hear, so the other students can hear, to be courteous to the person who is reading.

Listen.

Lesson 7. Replacing Books on Shelves

OBJECTIVES

1. To teach students the correct way to replace books on a shelf
2. To read a book to the class

MATERIALS

1. A book shelf with books or a few books between bookends
2. A book to read aloud. (For some suggestions, see Appendix D, "Books to Read Aloud.")

LESSON

Sometimes when students remove books from shelves, they don't replace them properly.

Today let's learn the correct way to put a book back on a shelf. First of all, when we put a book back on the shelf, we put it right side up with the spine facing out.

The spine is the part of the book you see when the book is shelved.

Point to the spine of a book: the 1 to 3 inch strip that joins the front and the back cover.

> The name of the book is on the spine. This book is _____.

> If the books were turned with open edges facing out, we wouldn't know which books they were.

Demonstrate.

> Sometimes when we put a book on the shelf, we catch another book inside our book. This can cause pages to be torn.

Demonstrate how one book can be caught inside another.

> Use your free hand to make an opening for the book before you put it on the shelf.

> Who would like to show us how to put a book back on the shelf?

Call on several students, one at a time, to demonstrate.

> We don't put a book on top of a row of books or on the outside of a bookend.

Inform the students that you are going to read a book to them.
Tell them that they should be quiet and still. If you need to, discuss the reasons: so they can hear, so the other students can hear, to be courteous to the person who is reading.

> Listen.

Read the book in an interesting way.
Praise the students for being quiet and still and for listening, if praise is deserved. If the students didn't behave well, discuss how they can improve their behavior.

SUGGESTIONS

If you have a school library,

1. Teach your students how to replace books on a shelf during your first library visit, in addition to any times this may have been taught previously.

2. Teach the students how to reshelve books every time your class visits the library.

3. Check to see what the reshelving policy is. Usually the librarian wants students to lay books on a table if they don't know where the books go. (Books shelved in the wrong places are lost books.) Teach your students what to do with books when they don't know where they should be reshelved.

Lesson 8. How to Turn Pages Properly

OBJECTIVES

1. To teach students how to turn pages
2. To read a book to the class

MATERIALS

1. A book with torn pages, if available (If one is not available, teach the lesson without it.)
2. A book for each student to use while practicing page turning (If the lesson is taught in the library, teach it at the end of the period so the library books the students check out can be used to practice page turning.)

LESSON

Inform the students that you are going to read a book to them.

Tell them that they should be quiet and still. If you need to, discuss the reasons: so they can hear, so the other students can hear, to be courteous to the person who is reading.

> Listen.

Read the book in an interesting way.

If you have a book with torn pages, show it to the students.

> Would you rather read a book with pages that have been torn or would you rather read a book that doesn't have torn pages?

> How do you think these pages got torn?

Whether or not you have a book with torn pages, teach the remainder of the lesson.

> Books have to be handled very carefully.

> If people turn pages at the bottom edge, the pages get torn.

> Pages get torn if they are turned quickly, too.

> We don't want to tear pages, so let's learn how to turn pages correctly.

> This is how we turn the pages of a book. We use the thumb and first finger of our right hand to turn a page.

Demonstrate.

> We hold the page at the top right corner. Then we slip our open hand behind the page and push the page forward.

> We always use our fingers to turn a page. We never use our palm.

Explain the meaning of palm.
See that each student has a book.

> Lay your book on the table right side up, facing you, as if you were going to read it.

Check to see that each book is right side up.
Demonstrate how to turn pages again.

> If you are left-handed, I'll give you special help in a few minutes.

> Everyone hold your right hand up.

Check to make sure that each child is holding up his or her right hand.

> Put your thumb and first finger at the top of the book. Pull the cover of the book forward a little, then slip your open hand behind the cover and push. Turn some pages now.

> I'm coming to watch each of you turn pages. Keep turning them.

Walk around the room. Pause and watch each individual student as he or she demonstrates the correct way to turn pages.

Try to get any left-handed students to use their right hands to turn pages. (Turning pages with the left hand is very awkward because the student can't put the hand behind a page to push. If students prefer using their left hands, show them the difficulties, but let them make the final decision.)

> Remember to always turn pages slowly at the top corner so they won't get torn.

Reteach this lesson periodically.

Lesson 9. Protecting Books from Nature

OBJECTIVES

1. To teach students to protect books from the dew, the rain, and the sun
2. To read a book to the class

MATERIALS

1. Books that have been damaged by the dew, the rain, or the sun, if they are available (If they are not available, teach the lesson without them.)
2. A plastic bag that is big enough to hold a book
3. A book to read aloud (For some suggestions, see Appendix D, "Books to Read Aloud.")

LESSON

We always take good care of books.

In the morning when we come to school, we don't lay our books on the wet, dewy grass while we play; the books will get wet and they may be permanently damaged.

If it's raining and we are carrying a book, we make sure that rain doesn't get on it. We carry the book in a plastic bag or inside our coat.

If you have a plastic bag, put a book into it for a graphic demonstration.

Did you know that the sun can hurt books? If you leave a book outside on a very hot day, your book will get warped.

If you have a warped book, show it to the class.

Warped means out of shape, damaged. Never leave a book in the sun.

If you leave a book in a car on a hot day, the cover of the book will get warped and the pages will be hurt. Never leave a book in a car on a hot day.

While we're talking of not leaving books in a car on a hot day, I want to mention something else, too. We never leave animals in a car on a hot day with the windows closed. The animals could die in just a few minutes. It gets much hotter in a closed car than it does outside. Never leave a book or an animal in a car on a hot day.

Inform the students that you are going to read a book to them.

Tell them that they should be quiet and still. If you need to, discuss the reasons: so they can hear, so the other students can hear, to be courteous to the person who is reading.

Listen.

Read the book in an interesting way.

Praise the students for being quiet and still and for listening, if praise is deserved. If the students didn't behave well, discuss how they can improve their behavior.

SUGGESTIONS

1. Keep a box for plastic bags in the classroom/library.
2. Have students provide bags from the supermarket, retail store, and so forth. (Be sure the bags are clean and dry.)
3. Encourage students to use these bags when taking books home.

Lesson 10. Using Bookmarks

OBJECTIVES

1. To teach the purpose of bookmarks
2. To teach what can be appropriately used for bookmarks
3. To read a book to the class

MATERIALS

1. A bookmark
2. A scrap of paper that would be suitable for a bookmark
3. A piece of scratch paper
4. A book to read aloud. (For some suggestions, see Appendix D, "Books to Read Aloud.")
5. Optional: A bookmark for each student (See Unit 3, Lesson 20, for some reproducible bookmarks.)

LESSON

Sometimes people want to mark the place where they are stopping in a book. Maybe the bell has rung for recess and some students haven't finished the books they are reading. They want to finish their books later. These students can mark their places with a bookmark.

Hold up a bookmark. Put it in a book and close the book to demonstrate its use.

If you don't have a fancy bookmark, you can use a small piece of paper for a bookmark.

Demonstrate.

A bookmark is thin and flat.

We never use a pencil for a bookmark. A pencil would hurt a book.

We don't dog-ear a book to save our place either. Dog-ear means to turn the top corner of a page down to mark your place.

Demonstrate with a piece of scratch paper.

Remember, when you want to mark your place, use a bookmark.

Inform the students that you are going to read a book to them.

Tell them that they should be quiet and still. If you need to, discuss the reasons: so they can hear, so the other students can hear, to be courteous to the person who is reading.

Read the book in an interesting way.

Praise the students for being quiet and still and for listening, if praise is deserved. If the students didn't behave well, discuss how they can improve their behavior.

If you plan to give bookmarks to the students, distribute them now.

SUGGESTIONS

1. You may want to give everyone a ditto-made bookmark and offer fancy bookmarks as rewards.
2. As an alternative, have students make their own bookmarks. (Coloring bookmarks with crayons is not recommended.)

Lesson 11. Introducing Fiction

OBJECTIVES

1. To instill an appreciation of books
2. To introduce the fact that some books aren't true
3. To read a fiction book to the class

MATERIAL

A worthwhile fiction book. (For some suggestions, see Appendix D, "Books to Read Aloud.")

LESSON

Inform the students that you are going to read a book to them.

Tell them that they are to be quiet and still during the story. If you need to discuss courteous behavior, do so.

Say that some books aren't true—they are made-up stories. State that the book you are going to read to them today is not true—it's made up. Tell them to listen and see if they like the story.

Read the book to the students.

> Did you like that book?

Explain that books are fun. They tell us all kinds of interesting stories.

> Books are good friends. No matter where we go, books are there.

> Books tell us about everything in the whole world. If you have a question, ask a book. We love books.

Praise the students for being quiet and still and for listening, if praise is deserved. If the students didn't behave well, discuss how they can improve their behavior.

Lesson 12. Introducing Nonfiction

OBJECTIVES

1. To instill an appreciation of books
2. To introduce the fact that some books are true
3. To read a nonfiction book to the class

MATERIAL

An easy nonfiction book. (Choose an interesting subject, such as spiders, snakes, lions, and so forth.)

LESSON

Inform the students that you are going to read a book to them.

Tell them that they are to be quiet and still while you are reading. If you need to discuss courteous behavior, do so.

Say that some books are true. State that the book you are going to read to them today is a true book. Tell them what the book is about.

Tell the students that you want them to listen carefully to see if they can learn one thing that they hadn't known before. Tell them that after you read the book, you will ask them what they learned.

Read the book.

Ask the students to tell you one thing they learned. Call on students who raise their hands.

Explain that books can teach us everything we want to know.

> Books can teach us how to take care of our pets, how to draw, how to cook. They can teach us all about animals, airplanes, and cars. They can teach us everything. If you have a question, ask a book.
>
> Books are good friends. They'll always be there for us. We love books.

Praise the students for being quiet and still and for listening, if praise is deserved. If the students didn't behave well, discuss how they can improve their behavior.

Lesson 13. Cultivating a Love of Books

OBJECTIVES

1. To cultivate a love of books
2. To introduce the students to good books
3. To expose the students to good illustrations
4. To read some just-for-fun books

MATERIAL

An appropriate book for the lesson you choose. (For some suggestions, see Appendix D, "Books to Read Aloud.")

LESSONS

Cover some or all of these lessons intermittently during the year.

1. Cultivate a love of books.

   a. Present enjoyable, appealing fiction.

   b. Present informational books of special interest.

   c. Treat the physical book with respect and tenderness and expect the students to do the same.

   d. Compliment books. For example, hug a book and say, "This book is such a good book. It made me happy to read it. I want to read it to you so you can enjoy it, too." After reading the book, look at it and say, "Thank you, book. That was a good story." Have a number of books in front of you. Say, "Books are good friends. No matter where you go, you'll have a friend because books are everywhere." Pick up several books and say, "Here's a friend. Here's another one and another one."

2. Read acclaimed standards.

3. Read other good books.

4. Read just-for-fun books.

5. Emphasize and discuss good illustrations.

6. Read books and discuss whether they are true or untrue, nonfiction or fiction.

7. Celebrate National Children's Book Week. This is a week set aside each year in November to promote reading among young people. Select an appropriate activity as your method of celebration from the following suggestions:

   a. Prior to National Children's Book Week, promise to read a book that you loved as a child. Read it during National Children's Book Week.

   b. Read one of the students' favorite books.

   c. Have the students make an illustration of a book they like or an illustration of the book you just read to them. Display the illustrations.

   d. Read a special book to the class.

   e. Give everyone a bookmark.

   f. Have a Book Fair to coincide with National Children's Book Week. (Invite teachers, parents, and students to buy books.)

   g. Let students create their own books and/or bookmarks.

UNIT 1

FIRST GRADE

What to Teach in First Grade

SUGGESTIONS

1. Before your first trip to the library, refer to Appendix A, "How to Conduct Library Visits."
2. You may want to use a green (go) marker and a red (stop) marker to designate the pages you need to teach.

LESSONS

Teach Lessons 1 through 13 in Unit K. These lessons cover such skills as book care and appreciation and library behavior, basic lessons from Unit K that need to be retaught. Lessons 14 through 18 teach listening skills and are specifically for first graders.

Listening Skills

Lesson 14. Listening Quietly to a Story

OBJECTIVES

1. To teach students to be quiet and still during a story
2. To teach students to listen
3. To read a book to the class

MATERIAL

A book to read aloud. (For some suggestions, see Appendix D, "Books to Read Aloud.")

LESSON

Tell the students that you are going to read a book to them.

Explain why they should be quiet and still—so they can hear, so the other students can hear, to be courteous to the person who is reading.

Hold up the book, with pictures facing the students.

> Listen.

Standing to the side of the book, read aloud in an interesting way.

Praise the students for being quiet and still and for listening, if praise is deserved. If the students didn't behave well, discuss how they can improve their behavior.

Lesson 15. Talking Without Words

OBJECTIVES

1. To teach students to be quiet and still during a story
2. To teach students to listen
3. To read a book to the class

MATERIAL

The book *Talking Without Words* by Marie Hall Ets (Viking, 1968). (If it is available, read it to yourself and consider whether your class would like it. If you think they would, read it to them. If you don't think so, read another book instead. While you're reading *Talking Without Words*, make a list of what your students could say without words and use your list in the lesson below.)

LESSON

Tell the students that you are going to read a book to them.

> Who remembers why we should be quiet and still when someone is reading?

Elicit responses such as: so they can hear, so the other students can hear, and to be courteous to the one who is reading.

Listen.

Read the book.

After the story, explain that you are going to tell the class something to do, and you want everyone to be quiet and still and to listen.

I'm going to tell you something to say, but you mustn't use your lips or voice. You may use your hands. Say, "Hello."

If one student gets the idea of waving, the others will see and wave, too. If no one responds, you wave. Then everyone should wave.

Say, "Come here."

The students should beckon with a finger. Show them if necessary.

Say, "I love you."

If the students don't know how to respond, help by throwing a kiss to them.

Say, "Be quiet."

The response should be a putting of the index finger on the lips.

Say, "Goodbye."

Students should wave.

Praise the students for being quiet and still and for listening, if praise is deserved. If the students didn't behave well, discuss how they can improve their behavior.

SUGGESTION

You may want to teach some symbols from the American Sign Language, which is a language of gestures used by the deaf and hearing impaired. Or you may want to teach some symbols from the sign language of the American Plains Indians.

Sources

American Sign Language

- Check your library's card catalog under the subject heading SIGN LANGUAGE.
- *The World Book Encyclopedia* has a picture of the American Manual Alphabet. See Sign Language.

- Bourke, Linda. *Handmade ABC: A Manual Alphabet.* Reading, Mass.: Addison Wesley, 1981.
- Sullivan, Mary Beth, and Linda Bourke. *A Show of Hands: Say It in Sign Language.* Reading, Mass.: Addison Wesley, 1980.

Indian Sign Language

- Check your library's card catalog under the subject heading INDIANS OF NORTH AMERICA—SIGN LANGUAGE. Some libraries may also have some references to Indian sign language under the subject heading SIGN LANGUAGE.
- *The World Book Encyclopedia* has nine small pictures illustrating Indian sign language. See Indian, American.
- Amon, Aline. *Talking Hands: Indian Sign Language.* New York: Doubleday, 1968.
- Hofsinde, Robert, *Indian Sign Language,* New York, Morrow, 1956.

Lesson 16. Listening to and Making Up Riddles

OBJECTIVES

1. To teach students to be quiet and still
2. To teach students to listen
3. To read a book to the class

MATERIAL

The book *It Does Not Say Meow and Other Animal Riddle Rhymes* by Beatrice Schenk de Regniers (Houghton Mifflin, 1983, paper). (If you can't obtain this book from your school or public library, ask your public librarian to try to get it for you through an interlibrary loan. If the book is unobtainable, you will have to skip this lesson. Note: The reference librarian at the public library will tell you over the phone if the library owns a particular book and if it is in.)

LESSON

Tell the students that you are going to read a book to them.
Explain that they are to sit still and listen.
Hold the book up as you tell the students its name.

> This is a book of riddles. It tells you all about something, but it doesn't tell you what that something is. You have to figure out what that something is. You have to figure out the answer to each riddle.

Hold the book the way you always hold picture books when reading them to a class—with the pictures facing the children. Standing at the side, read the first riddle aloud.

Call on students who are raising their hands until you get the correct answer. Then turn the page and hold the book up so the students can see the answer in picture form. Continue this procedure for the other riddles.

Praise the students for being quiet and still and for listening, if praise is deserved. If the students didn't behave well, discuss how they can improve their behavior.

FOLLOW-UP

Have a written and oral lesson on riddles. Start by reading a number of examples. Afterward, examine and discuss them. Put a riddle on the board and analyze it. Help the students see that riddles are made up of two parts: (1) clues that lead to a question and (2) an answer.

Tell a riddle. Let someone guess the answer. Discuss how the student figured out the answer. After numerous riddles have been examined and you are sure that the students comprehend the two essential parts, have the students write original riddles.

Tell the students that they must be still and listen when someone is sharing a riddle. Explain the reasons. They need to sit still and listen because this is courteous behavior when someone is speaking; this is being courteous to the speaker and to the students who are trying to hear. Explain that when they stand before the class to give their riddles, they will want everyone to be quiet and to listen. Therefore, they must do the same thing for other people. If they don't listen, they won't hear the riddles and won't be able to guess the answers.

Call on each student to come to the front of the class to read his or her riddle. Let the student choose someone to guess the answer.

At the conclusion of the lesson, comment about the interesting riddles that were shared. You may also want to put all of the riddles together in a class book. If you decide to do this, tell the students this prior to the writing of the riddles to increase their motivation.

Praise the students for being courteous, if they were. If they weren't courteous, discuss how they can improve their behavior.

Lesson 17. Listening for Something Special

OBJECTIVES

1. To teach students to be quiet and still during a story
2. To give students practice in listening for something special

MATERIAL

A book to read aloud. (For some suggestions, see Appendix D, "Books to Read Aloud.")

LESSON

Tell the students that you are going to read a book to them.

Review the reasons why they should be quiet and still—so they can hear, so the other students can hear, to be courteous to the person who is reading.

> As I read this book, I want you to listen very carefully because after the story I want you to tell the class which part you liked best.

Read the book.

> Which part of the story did you like best?

Call on those students who have their hands raised. Discuss any parts of the book that the students didn't mention.

Praise the students for being quiet and still and for listening, if praise is deserved. If the students didn't behave well, discuss how they can improve their behavior.

Lesson 18. A Listening Game

OBJECTIVES

1. To teach the students to listen
2. To read a book to the class
3. To play a listening game

MATERIAL

The book *Goodnight Moon* by Margaret Wise Brown (Harper and Row Junior Books, 1947). (If you are unable to obtain this book, select another title. For some suggestions, see Appendix D, "Books to Read Aloud.")

LESSON

Inform the students that you are going to read a book to them.

Ask them why they should be quiet and still while you're reading. Elicit answers such as *so they can hear, so the other students can hear, to be courteous to the person who is reading.*

Listen.

Read the book.

If you read *Goodnight Moon,* you may want to follow up with an oral lesson in which each child gets to say goodnight to something. Do it right after you read the story. Explain that the class is going to play a game in which they will be greeting not the moon, but the students in the room. And since it's not night, but morning/afternoon, they'll say good morning/afternoon. State that it's a game to which you have to listen very carefully.

If you did not read *Goodnight Moon,* introduce the game below by saying something like the following: Today we're going to play a game that will show you what good listeners you've become. Then explain and play the game.

Good Morning (Afternoon)

Have a student sit in the front of the room with his or her back to the class. Blindfold the student. (Alternative: Have the student cover his or her eyes.) Point to someone to come up behind and say, "Good morning (afternoon), _____ (name of student)." The person seated should return the greeting: "Good morning (afternoon), _____." If the person seated is correct in naming the other student, he or she may remain seated. If the student is not unseated by the next two greeters, give him or her a sticker, say that he or she is a very good listener, and have the student sit down. If the person seated does not identify the speaker correctly, remove the blindfold and have the student stand and shake the speaker's hand while saying, "Good morning, _____." Then the student may return to his or her seat. The student who unseated the blindfolded student sits in the seat.

UNIT 2

SECOND GRADE

What to Teach in Second Grade

SUGGESTIONS

1. Before your first trip to the library, refer to Appendix A, "How to Conduct Library Visits."
2. You may want to use a green (go) marker and a red (stop) marker to designate the pages you need to teach.

LESSONS

Teach Lessons 1 through 13 in Unit K and Lesson 19 in this unit. Lessons 1 through 13 teach skills such as book care and appreciation and library behavior, basic lessons from Unit K that need to be retaught. Lesson 19 teaches how to fill out a book card, a new skill for second graders.

Lesson 19. How to Fill Out a Book Card

OBJECTIVE

To teach students how to print their names on book cards

MATERIALS

1. A blank book card from the library
2. A book from the library to use in demonstrating the location of the book pocket and the book card

3. A chalkboard, chalk, and eraser

4. Make reproductions of the book cards at the end of this lesson. (Duplicate them on regular ditto paper. If your library's cards are different from both of the two cards pictured, make your own ditto.)

PREPARATIONS

1. Examine a book card from your library.

2. Copy the book card below on the chalkboard, modifying it to look like your library's cards. Use the names of two of your students instead of the two names listed to make the card more interesting. Notice that the first name is short and fits on one line. The second name is long and requires two lines. Substitutions should be similar in length.

3. Read this lesson to see if the procedures outlined are in accordance with your library's procedures. If not, modify the procedures in this lesson.

4. After making reproductions of the book cards at the end of this lesson, you may want to print each student's name on a separate card. This will provide a model for each student. If you don't want to do this, just pass the sample cards and let the students print without a model.

5. Put the blank book card that you got from the library into the pocket of your library book.

	Brown A cat for me	
Date	Name	
	Ann Wells 6	
	Johnny	
	Valentino 6	

LESSON

Teach this lesson just before a library visit.

> Today we're going to the library.
>
> Now that you're second graders, you won't need to have the librarian or teacher print your name for you when you check a book out. You may print your name yourself.
>
> Before we go to the library, you may practice filling out a card so you'll know just how to do it.

Pick up the library book and open it to the book pocket.
Demonstrate the following as you talk.

> A book pocket is inside the cover. Remove the book card from the pocket. Print your name and room number on the first empty line of the card.
>
> Let's look at the sample card I've put on the board.

Point to the board.

> The front of the card has typing on it. At the top is the name of the person who wrote the book.
>
> Who can read it? (Brown)
>
> On the next line we have the name of the book.
>
> Who can read it? (A Cat for Me)
>
> See the empty space where it says "Date"?

Point to the space labeled "Date."

> That is where the librarian will stamp the date by which you should return your book. Don't write in that space.
>
> The space to the right of the line is where you are to print your name and room number.
>
> Print very clearly. Remember to print your first and last name. Always include your room number.
>
> The name of the person who wrote the book and the name of the book are on the front of the book card.
>
> Print your name on the first empty line on the front of the card. Don't skip lines. If the front of the card is completely filled, turn to the back side and print on the first empty line.

Let's look at the names of the two people who have already checked this book out.

Who can read the first name?

That's a short name, isn't it?

Because it's so short, all of it was put on one line.

Notice that the room number is on the same line, too.

Look at the second name. It's a long name. It was necessary to use two lines to get it all down.

If you have a short name, try to get it on one line.

If you have a long name, use two lines.

I'm going to give a sample card to each of you.

If you have printed each student's name on a sample card, tell the students.

Find the first empty line, and print your first and last name and room number. If you have a long name, use two lines. Print clearly.

Be sure to leave a space between your first and last name. Leave a space between your last name and the room number, too.

I will come around to see if you are doing everything correctly. You may keep printing until I say stop.

Distribute the sample cards, which you have reproduced. Walk around and make sure that the students are printing their names as specified in the previous paragraphs. You will probably need to stress again and again that a space must be left between one's first and last name and before the room number. (Students tend to run the first name, the last name, and the room number together, which makes them very difficult to read.)

You did a good job.

When we go to the library, remember to print your first and last name and room number on the book card just like you did here in the classroom.

When you practiced today, you printed your name many times; in the library you will only print your name once.

I'm going to look at the cards you fill out in the library to see if you remember how to fill cards out correctly.

Let's get ready to go to the library.

Book Card Samples

If one of these cards is like the cards your library uses, make thirty-five to forty copies of this page, enough for all the students.

Cut out the cards you plan to use. A border will be all right, but explain to the students that they must stay within the card outline. Cut up the remainder for scrap paper.

If your library's cards are different from both of the ones below, you should make your own ditto.

Brown Cats, cats, cats	
Date	Name

Brown Cats, cats, cats		
Date	Name	Room

UNIT 3

THIRD GRADE

What to Teach in Third Grade

SUGGESTIONS

1. Before your first trip to the library, refer to Appendix A, "How to Conduct Library Visits."
2. If you have a slow third grade, which you feel would not be able to handle library skills, postpone the lessons until fourth grade.
3. You may want to use a green (go) marker and a red (stop) marker to designate the pages you need to teach.

LESSONS

Teach Lesson 20, "Book Care and Library Behavior," and Lesson 21, "Appreciating Books" (Third Through Sixth Grade). These concepts , which have been taught previously, need to be retaught. Teach Lessons 22A through 36, which are new to this grade level.

Lesson 20. Book Care and Library Behavior

OBJECTIVES

1. To teach the proper care of books
2. To teach appropriate library behavior
3. To teach students to assume responsibility for library materials

MATERIALS

1. A bookshelf with books or some books between bookends
2. Some books with torn pages or with writing, coloring, or other damage, if available
3. A book for each student to use when practicing page turning
4. Optional: A bookmark for each student (See the reproducible bookmarks at the end of this lesson.)

LESSON

This lesson is particularly appropriate immediately preceding a visit to the library. It might also precede the examination of some books in the classroom, or you may want to present it before reading a book to the class. It's a lesson that needs to be taught each year and reinforced constantly. You may choose to teach this lesson in two or more parts.

Everyone handles books. Let's review how we can take good care of them.

We should always have clean, dry hands when we handle books. We want to keep our books beautiful.

If we are going to put a book on a table, we should lay it down gently. We never slam books down. We have too much respect for the books and too much respect for the people we would disturb to do that.

Books aren't toys. We don't twirl them around or throw them.

We don't write or color on books. If you have an urge to write or color, get a piece of scratch paper. We want to keep our books clean and beautiful.

Books can get marked on accidentally if you put them in your desk next to some loose crayons or pencils. If possible, keep your crayons and pencils in a box. How else could you keep your books from getting marked accidentally?

If you take a book home, you should put it in a drawer or up high so your brothers, sisters, and pets can't get it.

We don't damage books in any way. Some books are damaged so badly by students that they have to be discarded. Books cost money. You might think to yourself, "The government will buy a new book." But the government has no money at all. If the government wants to buy something, it first has to take the money out of our pockets. Right now your fathers and mothers are the ones from whose pockets the government takes money, but someday when you are grown, the government will take the money from your pockets—the money to pay for all the damaged books, or for the broken school windows, or for the stolen equipment. Nothing is free. Everything has to come out of the pockets of the people. Take care of public property; it's *your* property. It was paid for with *your* money.

Demonstrate the following with books on a bookshelf or with books placed between bookends.

When you return a book to a library shelf, use your free hand to make room for the book you are shelving. This prevents catching a book inside your book.

Place the book right side up with the spine facing out.

Of course, you put the book in the right place. If you don't know the right place, don't shelve the book. Put it on the table.

What would happen if you shelved a book in the wrong place? (No one would be able to find it.)

If you need to mark your place in a book, use a bookmark or a small piece of scratch paper. Don't dog-ear a book. Dog-ear means to turn the corner down. Don't use a pencil to mark your place. A pencil hurts the book's spine. The glue or the threads that hold the book's pages together might be loosened and the pages might begin to fall out.

Books should be carried under your arm or against your chest. They should never be put on your head.

When you arrive at school in the morning, don't lay your books on the wet, dewy grass. The dampness will damage the books.

Never leave a book outside in the hot sun. The heat will warp the book; it will damage the cover and pages.

Never leave a book in a car on a hot day. The book will become warped. And while we're talking about cars and the hot sun, you know, of course, that one never leaves an animal in a car on a hot day. The animal could die within just a few minutes.

On a rainy day, be sure to carry your books in a plastic bag or carry them inside your coat.

When you use a library, you have certain responsibilities: (1) You should be quiet so other people can read or study; (2) you should put your chair back under the table before leaving the library; (3) you are responsible to take care of the books you borrow; (4) you should return books on time; and (5) if you are going to move away, you should return any library books you have before you move.

To turn the pages of a book, use the thumb and forefinger. Hold the page at the top right corner. Slip your open hand behind the page and push the page forward. Let's see you practice. Take a book out and turn the pages. I'm going to walk around the room and check to see if each one of you knows how to turn the pages in a book.

If you always turn pages slowly and gently at the top right corner, book pages won't get torn.

When you get a new book, you should always limber it up before reading it. *To limber a book* means to make it less stiff. Librarians usually call limbering "opening a new book."

Here's how to open a new book. Hold the book with its spine touching the table. Then open the front cover until it touches the table. Keep the pages of the book upright in one hand. With the index finger of your free hand, rub back and forth along the gutter where the pages are sewn together. Then open the back cover. Rub back and forth along the gutter. Take a few pages, ten or twelve, from the front of the book and lay them down. With the index finger of your free hand, rub back and forth along the gutter. Now take a few pages from the back of the book and lay them down. Rub your finger back and forth in the gutter. Continue taking a few pages from the back and a few pages from the front until all of the pages have been limbered.

Let's practice "opening a book" together.

See that each student has a book. Repeat the steps above orally and physically. Check to see that the students are doing the limbering properly.

When you get a new book, you'll know how to open it, how to limber it up.

Have the students put the books away.
If you plan to give bookmarks to the students, distribute them now.
Proceed with the follow-up activity that you have planned.

SUGGESTION

If you have any left-handed students, try to get them to use their right hands to turn pages. Turning pages with the left hand is very awkward because students can't put their left hands behind a page to push. If the left-handed students prefer using their left hands, show them the difficulties, but let them make the final decision.

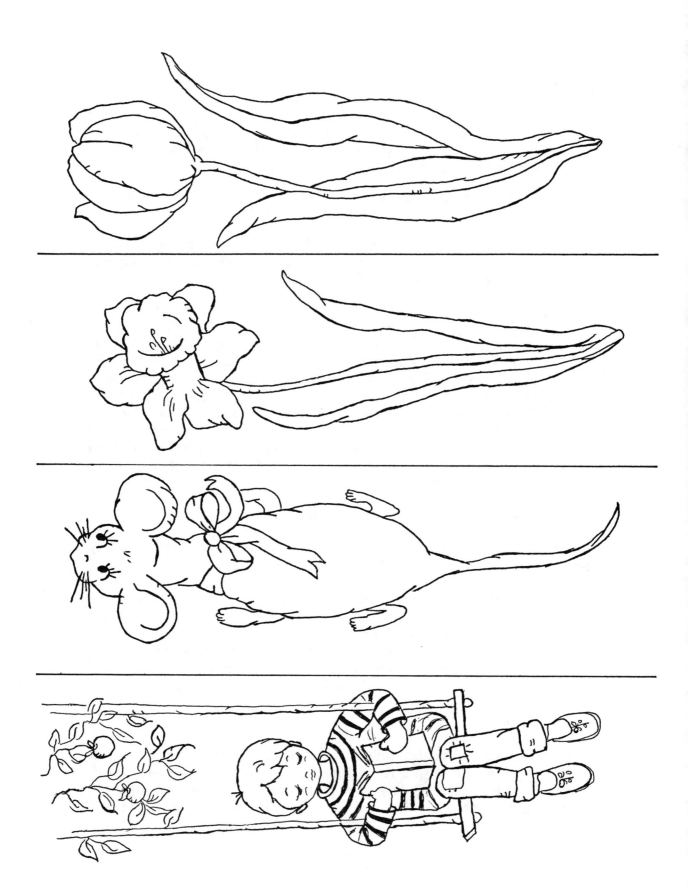

Lesson 21. Appreciating Books
(Third Through Sixth Grade)

OBJECTIVES

1. To cultivate a love of books
2. To instill an appreciation of good content
3. To instill an appreciation of good illustrations
4. To introduce book awards
5. To read various forms of the written word: books, short stories, poems, limericks, jokes, riddles
6. To introduce and read some just-for-fun books

LESSON IDEAS

Use some of these lesson ideas intermittently during the year.

Third and Fourth Grades

Teach the students about the Caldecott medal. See the section on the Caldecott Medal Winners in Appendix J, "Award-Winning Books." Choose from the following activities. (Third grade teachers, this lesson would be most appropriate after Lesson 24, "Illustrations.")

1. Read a Caldecott winner and show the illustrations as you read.
2. Show illustrations from several Caldecott award winners.
3. If you have a library, have the librarian pull the Caldecott winners for you to check out. Put the books in a learning center. Tell the students to examine the pictures and to pick out the book whose illustrations they like best. Use this information in one of the following ways:
   a. Have the students show their favorite illustrations and tell specifically what makes the illustrations appealing.
   b. Conduct a hand-count vote for the most popular illustrations. If you record the results on the chalkboard, you can bring in some math concepts. Ask: Which book got the most votes? Ask: How many more votes did it get than the closest runner-up? Have someone do the last problem on the board. This student should tell whether the answer was obtained by adding or subtracting. (subtracting)
   c. Reproduce some graphs and let the students chart hand votes. Tie in some math concepts. Ask: Which book got the most votes? Ask: How many more votes did it get than the closest runner-up? Have someone do the last problem on the board.

Third to Sixth Grade

1. Celebrate National Children's Book Week. This is a week set aside each year in November to promote reading among young people. Select an appropriate activity from this unit as your method of celebration.

2. Read some award-winning books. *Children's Books: Awards and Prizes,* published by The Children's Book Council, Inc., 67 Irving Place, N.Y., N.Y. 10003, lists four award categories. They are U.S. awards selected by adults, U.S. awards selected by young readers, British Commonwealth awards, and international and multinational awards. Of special interest, in the U.S. awards selected by young readers section, is the listing of state awards. Twenty-eight states and their awards are listed.

3. Read one or more books from "Children's Choices," a list of newly published books that children like and have selected. The list is published annually in the October issue of the International Reading Association's magazine, *The Reading Teacher.*

4. Read some of the winners of Raintree Publishing Company's annual Publish-a-Book Contest. Fourth, fifth, and sixth grade teachers/librarians may want to have their students participate in the contest. See Appendix I, "Publish-a-Book Contest."

5. If you have a library that has biographical books about authors and illustrators such as *Something About the Author* or *Children's Literature from A to Z,* have your students give oral or written reports on their favorite authors or illustrators. See Lesson 67.

6. Have the students write letters to their favorite authors or illustrators. See Appendix H for a list of authors and illustrators and their addresses. Precede this activity with lessons on letter-writing skills.

7. Have your students make posters about books and reading.

8. Let your students design original bookmarks. Give awards for the best ones. Duplicate the award-winning bookmarks and present them to one or more classes.

9. Round up a number of copies of a good book and let one or all of your reading groups read it.

10. Read, review, or introduce other good books to your students.

11. Present other good illustrations.

12. Read some just-for-fun books.

13. Read poems, limericks, jokes, and riddles to your students.

14. Invite an author or illustrator to speak to your student body.

Fifth and/or Sixth Grades

1. Introduce the Newbery medal (see section on Newbery Medal Winners in Appendix J, "Award-Winning Books").

2. Read a chapter a day from a Newbery winner.

3. Introduce or review a number of Newbery award winners. If you have a librarian, maybe he or she will do this for you.

4. If you have a library, have the librarian pull the Newbery winners for you to check out. Put the books on a table in the classroom. Let students select one book to read. (Alternative: Ask the librarian to pull the books and have them ready to put on a table for your class at your next visit.)

5. Assign either written or oral reports, if desired. Precede reports with instructions on mechanics. For points to teach, plus oral and written report reproducibles, see lessons 35 and 36.

SUGGESTIONS

1. Have a bulletin board display of book jackets of Caldecott and/or Newbery award winners.

2. Feature a picture and/or a short biographical sketch of an author or illustrator on the bulletin board. Recommended source: *Schooldays*, 19771 Magellan Drive, Torrance, California 90502.

Lesson 22A. The Book Cover, Part I

(For schools with libraries. If you don't have a library, see Lesson 22B.)

OBJECTIVES

1. To teach students to find the name of a book on the book's cover

2. To teach students to find, on the book's cover, the name of the person who wrote the book

3. To provide free reading time that includes teacher assistance

MATERIAL

A library book for each student

LESSON

NOTE: The words *title* and *author* are introduced in Lesson 23A.
Hold a student's library book up and point to the title on the cover.

_____ (student's name) checked out a book named
_____.

Who would like to tell me the name of the book he or she checked out?

Call on individual students to read the names of their books.

Everyone hold up your book so I can see it.

Point to the name of your book.

Check to see that each student is pointing to the name of the book.

Hold up the book whose title you have just read, and point to the author's name.

This book was written by _____.

Who can tell me who wrote your book?

Call on individual students.

Everyone hold up your book, so I can see it. Point to the name of the person who wrote it.

Check to see that each student is pointing to the name of the author.

Tell the students that you are going to give them some time to read their library books. Ask them to raise their hands if they need help.

Walk around the room and help students with the words they can't read. If you need a helper, choose your best reader to assist.

Conclude the reading activity after ten minutes.

SUGGESTIONS

1. The ten minutes of free reading time, as outlined above, could be a follow-up to each library visit or it could be a daily activity.
2. As a daily activity, you might want to schedule it right after lunch or recess. Students could enter the room, sit down, and start reading without having to be instructed daily to do so.

Lesson 22B. The Book Cover, Part I

(For schools without libraries. If you have a library, use Lesson 22A.)

OBJECTIVES

1. To teach students to find the name of a book on the book's cover
2. To teach students to find, on the book's cover, the name of the person who wrote the book
3. To read a book to the class

MATERIALS

1. A library book for each student or several library books that you can use for demonstration
2. A library book to read aloud to the class
3. Students' textbooks

LESSON

NOTE: The words *title* and *author* are introduced in Lesson 23B.

Try to provide a book for each student from a classroom library, the school district's library, or the public library. If you are able to do this, teach Lesson 22A instead of this lesson. If you are not able to do this, obtain a few books that you can show to the students.

> I have several books that I'd like to show you.

Hold up a book and point to its title.

> The name of this book is _____.

Hold up several other books, one at a time, and call on students to read the names of the books.

Present the books again. This time pick up a book and point to the author's name.

> The name of the person who wrote this book is _____.

Pick up a second book and ask who wrote it.
Hold up the other books, one at a time, and ask who wrote each of them.

> Take out your math book and hold it up so I can see it.

> Point to the name of the book.

Check to see if the students are pointing correctly.

Who would like to read the name of the book?

Point to the name of the person who wrote the book.

Who would like to read the person's name?

Ask the students to take out their other textbooks. Have them identify the books' names and the people who wrote the books.

Put your books away.

Pick up the book you plan to read aloud.

I think you might enjoy this book named _____, which was written by _____.

Read the book.

Lesson 23A. The Book Cover, Part II

(For schools with libraries. If you don't have a library, use Lesson 23B instead.)

OBJECTIVES

1. To teach the meaning of the words *title* and *author*
2. To teach the correct pronunciation of *author*
3. To provide free reading time, including teacher assistance

MATERIAL

A library book for each student

LESSON

Hold a student's library book up and point to the title on the cover. Tell the students the name of the book and tell them who checked it out.

Instead of saying the name of this book is _____, I could say the title of this book is _____. The word *title* means "name."

Who would like to read the title of your book?

Call on students to respond.

Hold up your books so I can see them.

Point to the title.

Hold up the book whose title you read, and point to the author's name.

The name of the person who wrote this book is _____.
Instead of saying the person who wrote this book is _____, I
could say the author of this book is _____. The word *author*
means "person who wrote the book."

Who would like to read the name of your author?

Explain that the word *author* is pronounced *au*thor, not *Ar*thur. Arthur is a
boy's name. Ask the class to say *au*thor together.

Hold up your book so I can see it.

Point to the author.

Check to see that each student is pointing correctly.

What is a title? (the name of a book)

What is an author? (a person who writes a book)

Tell the students that you are going to give them time to read their library
books. Ask them to raise their hands if they need help.
Walk around the room and help students with the words they can't read. If you
need a helper, choose your best reader to assist.
Conclude the reading activity after ten minutes.

SUGGESTION

Use the words *author* and *title* at every opportunity throughout the year.

Lesson 23B. The Book Cover, Part II

(For schools without libraries. Schools with libraries should use Lesson 23A.)

OBJECTIVES

1. To teach the meaning of the words *title* and *author*
2. To teach the correct pronunciation of *author*
3. To read a book to the class

MATERIALS

1. A library book for each student or several library books that you can hold
    up for demonstration

    2. A library book to read aloud to the class

    3. Students' textbooks

LESSON

Try to provide a book for each student. If you are able to do this, teach Lesson 23A instead of this lesson. If you are not able to do this, obtain a few books that you can show the students.

> I have several books that I'd like to show you.

Hold up a book and point to its title.

> The name of this book is _____. Instead of saying the name of this book is _____, I could say the title of this book is _____. The word *title* means "name."

Point to the author's name.

> The name of the person who wrote this book is _____. Instead of saying the person who wrote this book is _____, I could say the author of this book is _____. The word *author* means the "person who wrote the book."
>
> Author is pronounced *au*thor, not *Ar*thur. Arthur is a boy's name.

Ask the students to say *au*thor together.
Hold up another book.

> Who can read the title of this book?

Point to the author.

> Who can read the author's name?

Continue with several books.

> Take out your math book.
>
> Hold it up so I can see it.
>
> Point to the title.

Check to see that each student is pointing correctly.

> Who would like to read the title?
>
> Point to the author.

Check to see that each student is pointing correctly.

Who would like to read the name of the author?

Continue this identification of title and author with some other textbooks.

What is a title? (the name of a book)

What is an author? (a person who writes a book)

Put your books away.

Hold up one of the books that you introduced earlier.

I think you might enjoy this book titled _____. The author is _____.

Read the book to the class.

Lesson 24. Illustrations

OBJECTIVES

1. To introduce students to good illustrations
2. To teach the meaning of the words *illustrations* and *illustrator*

MATERIALS

1. A selection of books with particularly attractive illustrations. (See Appendix E, "Illustrations to Share.")
2. A chalkboard, chalk, and eraser
3. Optional: See Appendix F, "Illustrators' Styles and Characteristics," if you would like to refer to some descriptions of illustrators' styles and characteristics.

PREPARATION

Write these words on the chalkboard, lined up letter by letter as presented here:

illustrations
illustrator

LESSON

You recently learned two new words relating to books. The first one is a word that means name of a book.

Who can tell me what it is? (title)

The second new word you learned is a word that means the person who wrote the book.

Who can tell me what it is? (author)

Today you are going to learn two more new words. These words are related to the pictures in a book. The first one is a word that means pictures. It is *illustrations*.

Hold up a book with the pictures facing the students.

You could say there are pictures in this book. Or you could say there are illustrations in this book. Pictures and illustrations are the same thing.

The person who creates the illustrations is called an *illustrator*.

I've put the words *illustrations* and *illustrator* on the board.

Underline the similar parts of the two words.

illustrations
illustrator

Do you see how the two words are alike except for the endings?

This is an indication that the meanings are related. The first word means "pictures," and the second word means "a person who draws pictures."

I've brought some books with beautiful illustrations to share with you.

This book, titled _____, has very attractive illustrations.

Show a few of the pictures.

The person who drew the pictures, the illustrator, is _____.

Show the illustrations from several books. Give the title and illustrator for each. Be sure to use the words *title, illustrations,* and *illustrator* as frequently as possible.

I'm going to leave these books out so you can examine the illustrations more closely. You may read the books, too, of course.

FOLLOW-UP

1. This would be an appropriate time to teach one or more lessons about the Caldecott medal. See Lesson 21.

2. Have your students write books. Let them choose classmates to illustrate them. Use the words *author, title, illustrator,* and *illustrations* as much as

possible. Call the students *authors* when they are writing. Call the artists *illustrators*. Refer to the illustrations by name frequently.

Lesson 25. The Title Page, Part I

OBJECTIVES

1. To teach the following parts of a title page: the title, the author, the illustrator, the publisher, and the place of publication
2. To introduce and develop an understanding of copyrights

MATERIALS

1. A book with a simple, one-page title page
2. A chalkboard, chalk, and eraser
3. One or more sheets of typing paper

LESSON

Open a book to the title page, and hold it up for the class to see.

There is an important page in the front of a book called a *title page*.

What one thing would you expect to find on the title page? (the title)

What is a title? (the name of a book)

To help your class relate to the following example, designate one of your students to be an author. Use this student's name instead of the word *author* that appears throughout this example.

Let's pretend that _____ (student) has written a book.

Draw an outline of a title page on the board.
Ask the student author to state the title of his or her book.
Write the title inside the chalkboard outline. (See Worksheet 3.1 at the end of Lesson 26 for an example of title page form.)

Who is the author?

Under the title, write: by _____ (student author).
State that the class needs to know how a book comes into being. Explain that after the author wrote the book, he or she had someone type it up. Next, the author had to establish the fact that he or she was the author in order to receive any money that the book earned. The author didn't want anyone to be able to steal the ideas in

the book. For protection, the author applied for a copyright. He or she sent a copyright form, $10, and one copy of the book to the Copyright Office in Washington, D. C. The copyright that the author received established the fact that he or she was the legal owner of the book. No one may lawfully copy the book without the author's permission.

One definition of a copyright is "the exclusive right to publish, produce, or sell one's book, play, etc." Explain the word *exclusive*. Another definition of copyright is "proof of ownership of a book, play, or other literary work."

> The fact that a book has been copyrighted is usually printed on the back side of the title page.

> The copyright notice will look like one of these.

In a separate area on the board, write:

> Copyright 1986
> © 1986

> If the author got the copyright after January 1, 1978, the copyright will protect the book for his or her lifetime plus fifty years.

> The author will send a copy of the book to a number of publishers to find one who is interested in publishing the book. The publisher may send the author an advance payment. After the book is published, the author will probably receive royalties, payment based upon how many books are sold.

> The publisher will assign an illustrator to draw pictures for the book. Later the publisher will send the typed pages and the illustrations to the printer and a book will be the result.

Hold up some sheets of typing paper and then hold up a hardback book to demonstrate the book's progress.

> The publisher will send copies of the book to bookstores throughout the country.

> Let's pretend that Random House is the publisher who has agreed to publish the book.

Write Random House at the bottom of the chalkboard title page.

> Random House will appear at the bottom of the title page.

> The place of publication will appear under the publisher's name.

Write New York on the board under Random House.

Explain that the place of publication is the name of the city where the book was made. Some publishing companies have offices in several cities. In such cases, more than one city will be named.

Random House's books are published in New York.

The title page is finished except for one thing. We need to include the name of the illustrator.

Who remembers what an illustrator does? (creates the pictures for a book)

Let's pretend that the pictures were drawn by _____ (student artist in your room).

On the chalkboard, underneath the author's name, write: illustrated by _____ (student artist).

I'd like to see if you understand the parts of a title page.

Ask these questions:

1. Who is the author?
2. What is the title of the book?
3. Where is the place of publication? (New York)
4. Who is the publisher? (Random House)
5. Who drew the pictures?
6. Where is a title page located in a book? (in the front)

Lesson 26. The Title Page, Part II

OBJECTIVES

1. To present two title pages
2. To review the parts of a title page
3. To review the meaning of copyright
4. To check comprehension with a follow-up ditto

MATERIALS

1. Back-to-back reproductions of Worksheets 3.1 and 3.2. (Paper-saving alternative: Copy the two worksheets onto the board.)
2. Reproductions of Worksheet 3.3
3. A chalkboard, chalk, and eraser

LESSON

Today we're going to examine two title pages.

Pass out the back-to-back reproductions of Worksheets 3.1 and 3.2. (Students are not to write on these pages.)

Look at Worksheet 3.1.

Call on a student who has a loud, clear voice to read the entire page. Ask these questions about Worksheet 3.1.

1. What is a title? (a name of a book)
2. What is the title of this book? (*How to Draw Animals*)
3. What is an author? (a person who writes a book)
4. Who is the author of this book? (Dan Johnson)
5. What is a publisher? (the company that has the book made and sells it)
6. Who is the publisher of this book? (John Smith Publishing Company)
7. What does place of publication mean? (where the book was published)
8. Where was this book published? (New York)
9. What are illustrations? (pictures)
10. What is an illustrator? (a person who creates a book's pictures)
11. Who is the illustrator? (Ann Brown)
12. In what part of a book is a title page found? (in the front)

Now turn your dittos over.

Ask these questions about Worksheet 3.2:

1. Where was the book published? (Chicago)
2. Who illustrated the book? (Bill Long)
3. Who is the author? (John Miles)
4. What is the title? (*The Last Dinosaur*)
5. Who is the publisher? (Lighthouse Press)
6. Who remembers what a copyright is? (A copyright is an exclusive right to publish, produce, or sell one's book, play, etc.)

I'm going to distribute a ditto for you to fill out.

Pass out reproductions of Worksheet 3.3.
Correct the dittos with the students or collect, correct, and return them later.

How to Draw Animals

by Dan Johnson

pictures by Ann Brown

John Smith Publishing Company
New York

The Last Dinosaur

by John Miles

illustrated by Bill Long

Lighthouse Press
Chicago

Worksheet 3.3 The Title Page

The New Girl

by Janet Clark

drawings by Ray Black

New Books
New York

1. Who is the illustrator? _____

2. What is the title? _____

3. Who is the author? _____

4. Where was the book published? _____

5. Who is the publisher? _____

Lesson 27. The Title Page, Part III

OBJECTIVES

1. To introduce a two-page title page
2. To present a half title page
3. To present a title page that features two authors
4. To check comprehension with a follow-up ditto

MATERIALS

1. A book with a title page that extends across two pages (See "References" section at the end of this lesson for some suggestions.)
2. A book with a half title page (See "References" section at the end of this lesson for some suggestions.)
3. Back-to-back reproductions of Worksheets 3.4 and 3.5 (located at the end of this lesson)

LESSON

Open a book that has a title page extending across two pages. Show it to the class as you say the following:

> A title page features a book's title, author, illustrator, publisher, and place of publication.

> Sometimes instead of just occupying one page, a title page is spread across two pages.

Open a book to a half title page. Show it to the class as you say the following:

> Some books have a half title page in addition to a title page. A half title page features only the book's title. If a book has a half title page, it will be found right before the title page.

> I am going to distribute a double-sided ditto.

Pass out back-to-back reproductions of Worksheets 3.4 and 3.5. Worksheet 3.4 is for oral presentation. Worksheet 3.5 is a follow-up ditto.

> Look at Worksheet 3.4.

> Who would like to read the entire page?

Ask these questions:

1. Who is the publisher of this book? (Sunshine Press)
2. What is a publisher? (the company that produces and sells a book)
3. What are illustrations? (pictures)
4. Who is the illustrator? (Mike Parks)
5. Who is Alan Baker? (the author)
6. What is an author? (a person who writes a book)
7. Where was the book published? (Boston)
8. What is the title? (*Crafts for You*)
9. What does the word *title* mean? (the name of a book)
10. Who is James West? (a co-author *or* a second author)

> Turn your ditto over. Write your name and today's date at the top, and then complete the page.

Correct the papers with the students or collect, correct, and return them later.

REFERENCES

Each of the following books features both a two-page title page and a half title page:

> *The Girl Who Loved Wild Horses,* Paul Goble
>
> *Tico and the Golden Wings,* Leo Lionni
>
> *Where the Wild Things Are,* Maurice Sendak

Crafts for You

Alan Baker and James West

decorations by Mike Parks

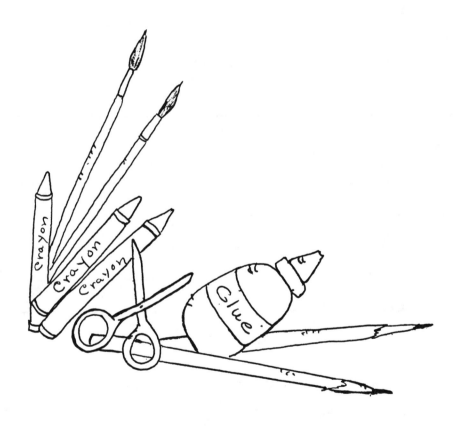

Sunshine Press
Boston

Name _____ Date _____

Worksheet 3.5 The Title Page

Animals You Know

written and illustrated by Jane Dickson

Children's Books
San Francisco

Answer these:

1. Who is the author? _____

2. What is the title? _____

3. Who is the publisher? _____

4. Who is the illustrator? _____

5. Where was the book published? _____

Match these:

6. _____ company that has a book printed and then has it sold   a. author

7. _____ person who draws the pictures for a book   b. title

8. _____ person who writes a book   c. publisher

9. _____ name of a book   d. illustrator

10. _____ place where a book is published   e. place of
                                                                          publication

Lesson 28. The Title Page, Part IV

OBJECTIVES

1. To review a half title page
2. To review a title page
3. To guide students in defining the parts of a title page
4. To direct the students in the location of a title page

MATERIALS

1. Back-to-back reproductions of Worksheets 3.6 and 3.7 (Paper-saving alternative: Copy the two pages on the board.)
2. A library book or textbook for each student

LESSON

Inform the students that you are going to review a half title page and a title page. Pass the double-sided ditto out.

Ask the students to examine both sides of the ditto. When they find the half title page, they are to hold it up facing you.

Check to see if everyone has found the correct side.

> If the words "half title page" weren't printed at the top, how would you know that was the half title page? (The only written information is the title.)

> Turn the page over.

Ask the following questions:

1. What do we call this page? (a title page)
2. Who is the illustrator? (June Day)
3. Where was the book published? (New York)
4. Who is the author? (Tim Williams)
5. What is the title? (*Books for You*)
6. Who is the publisher? (Little Press)

Collect the dittos.
Ask the following questions:

1. What does place of publication mean? (where a book was published)
2. What is an author? (a person who writes a book)

3. What is an illustrator? (a person who creates the pictures for a book)
4. What is a title? (the name of a book)
5. What is a publisher? (a company that produces and sells a book)
6. What is a copyright? (an exclusive right to publish, produce, or sell one's book *and* proof that one owns the rights to a book)
7. Where is a title page located? (in the front of a book)
8. What are illustrations? (pictures)

Tell the students to take a library book out of their desks. If library books aren't available, use textbooks.

During the following activity, walk around the room and check each student's identification of each part of the title page. For example, say, "Find the title page in your book. Touch the title." Then walk quickly around the room and check each student's title. Say, "Touch the name of the author." Walk quickly around the room again and check each student. Continue through each part of the title page. Give the following instructions:

1. Find the title page in your book. (If someone has found a half title page by mistake, ask the class how one can tell the difference between a half title page and a title page.)
2. Point to the title.
3. Point to the name of the author.
4. Point to the name of the illustrator.
5. Point to the name of the publisher.
6. Point to the place of publication.
7. Find the copyright notice. Touch it. The copyright notice is on the back of the title page.

After a word of praise, ask your students to put their books away.

Books for You

Worksheet 3.6 The Half Title Page

Books for You

Tim Williams

illustrated by June Day

Little Press
New York

Lesson 29. The Title Page, Part V

OBJECTIVES

1. To review two title pages
2. To guide the students in defining the parts of a title page and in defining copyright
3. To direct the students in the location of a title page and a copyright notice
4. To check mastery of the lesson with a follow-up ditto

MATERIALS

1. Back-to-back reproductions of Worksheets 3.8 and 3.9 (Paper-saving alternative: Copy the two worksheets onto the board.)
2. A library book or a textbook for each student (If students have only the library books they used in their last lesson, they can exchange books with one another.)
3. Back-to-back reproductions of Worksheets 3.10 and 3.11

LESSON

Today we're going to review title pages.

Pass out the back-to-back reproductions of Worksheets 3.8 and 3.9.

Look at Worksheet 3.8.

Ask these questions:

1. Where was this book published? (New York)
2. Who is the illustrator? (Ward King)
3. Who is the publisher? (Western Press)
4. Who is the author? (David Martin)
5. What is the title? (*Starlight, Starbright: Poems About America*)

   The part after the colon is part of the title, too. It's a *subtitle*—a secondary title used to explain what *Starlight, Starbright* is about. The whole title of the book is *Starlight, Starbright: Poems About America*.

   Now turn the page over to Worksheet 3.9.

Ask these questions:

1. Who are Dale Cook and Jill Wilson? (authors of the book)
2. Who published the book? (Three Rivers Press)

3. Where was the book published? (San Francisco)
4. What is the title? (*Crocodiles and Alligators*)
5. Who is the illustrator? (Joe Robinson)

Collect the papers.

Ask these questions:

1. What is a title? (the name of a book)
2. What is an author? (a person who writes a book)
3. What is a publisher? (a company that produces and sells a book)
4. What is an illustrator? (a person who creates the pictures for a book)
5. What does place of publication mean? (where the book was published)
6. What is a copyright? (proof of ownership of a book, play, etc., *and* an exclusive right to publish, produce, and sell a book)
7. Where is the title page located in a book? (in the front)
8. Where is the copyright notice found? (on the back of the title page)
9. How can you tell a half title page from a title page? (A half title page has only the book's title.)

Ask students to take a library book out of their desks. If they have only the book that they used for the last lesson, let them exchange books with one another. If library books are not available, use textbooks.

During the following activity, walk around the room and check each student on each identification of title page parts.

Say:

1. Find the title page.
2. Is there a half title page?
3. Find the title of your book. Point to it.
4. Who would like to read the title?
5. Find the author's name. Point to it.
6. Who would like to read the author's name?
7. Find the illustrator's name. Point to it.
8. Who would like to read the illustrator's name?
9. Find the publisher's name. Point to it.
10. Who would like to read the name of the publisher?
11. Find the place of publication. Point to it.
12. Who would like to read the place of publication?
13. Find the copyright date. Point to it.
14. Who would like to read the copyright date?

Tell the students to put their books away.

You've learned a great deal about title pages and copyrights. I'm going to distribute a ditto for you to do. It will tell you how much you remember of what you've learned.

Pass out copies of Worksheets 3.10 and 3.11, reproduced back to back. Students may look at the title page printed on Worksheet 3.10 to help them place the parts of their own title page on Worksheet 3.11.

As soon as you get your paper, you may start to work.

Collect the papers, grade them, and determine whether the subject matter has been mastered sufficiently for the grade level. If mastery is insufficient, you may want to do further drill work before going on to the next subject in this manual.

Note that there are twenty items on the test.

To enable you to check the student-made title page quickly, the parts are placed in alphabetical order:

> <u>A</u>ll About Fish
> <u>B</u>ill Parker
> <u>C</u>andy Miller
> <u>D</u>awson Company
> <u>E</u>ngland

To check the other items, see Appendix C, Worksheet Answers.

SUGGESTIONS

1. You may want to have your students write a book, which would include a title page.
2. If so, put a model title page on the board for the students or let them use Worksheets 3.8 and 3.9.

Starlight, Starbright: Poems about America

David Martin

illustrated by Ward King

Western Press
New York

Crocodiles and Alligators

Dale Cook and Jill Wilson

illustrated by Joe Robinson

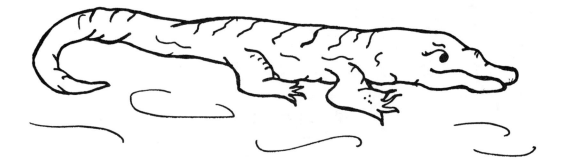

Three Rivers Press
San Francisco

Worksheet 3.10 The Title Page

Swinging on a Star

Frank Walker

pictures by Nan Hall

Bluebird Press
New York

1. Who is the illustrator? _____

2. Who is the author? _____

3. What is the title? _____

4. Who is the publisher? _____

5. Where is the place of publication? _____

6. Is this a half title page or a title page? _____

7. Is the copyright notice found on the front or on the back of the title page? _____

    _____

8. Are illustrations books, pictures, or authors? _____

Name _____   Date _____

Worksheet 3.11 The Title Page

Match these:

_____ 1. title   a. a person who draws pictures for a book

_____ 2. author   b. the name of a book

_____ 3. illustrator   c. a person who writes a book

_____ 4. publisher   d. a page which has only the book's title printed on it

_____ 5. place of publication   e. the company that makes and sells a book

_____ 6. copyright   f. where a book is published

_____ 7. half title page g. proof that one owns a book

Make a title page using the following information:

Author,   Bill Parker
Title,   All about Fish
Publisher,   Dawson Company
Illustrator,   Candy Miller
Place of publication,   England

Lesson 30. The Table of Contents, Part I

OBJECTIVES

1. To introduce the table of contents
2. To present two tables of contents for study
3. To check comprehension with a follow-up ditto

MATERIALS

1. A book of fairy tales containing a table of contents
2. A fiction book containing only one story
3. Back-to-back reproductions of Worksheets 3.12 and 3.13
4. A library book or textbook for each student
5. A reproduction of Worksheet 3.14

LESSON

Hold up a book of fairy tales that contains a table of contents.

Explain that the book has a number of stories in it.

There is a list of the stories in the front of the book. The list is called a *table of contents.*

Turn to the table of contents.

Hold the book up for the students to see.

Turn the book to yourself and look down the page.

> I'm looking for the story called "Cinderella," but it isn't in this book.

> The table of contents tells us what's in a book. By looking at a table of contents, we can decide if we want a book or not.

> The table of contents also tells us on which page each story or chapter begins.

Hold up a fiction book containing one story.

> A fiction book with only one story doesn't usually have a table of contents. Occasionally, though, a fiction book lists the titles of its chapters on a contents page.

> I'm going to pass out a double-sided ditto on which you'll find two tables of contents.

Distribute the reproductions of Worksheets 3.12 and 3.13.

Look at Worksheet 3.12.

Who would like to read the names of the chapters?

Ask these questions:

1. What is this book about? (pets *or* animals)
2. How many chapters are in the book? (6)
3. Would you want to check this book out of the library if you were looking for information about snakes? (no)
4. Are the chapters arranged in alphabetical order? (no)
5. In what order are the chapters arranged? (in the order that they appear in the book)
6. What is the second chapter about? (dogs)
7. On what page does the chapter on birds begin? (page 31)
8. On what page does it end? (page 38)
9. What is the title of the chapter that begins on page 39? (Mice)
10. On what page does the chapter on fish end? (We don't know; the table of contents doesn't say.)

Turn the ditto over to Worksheet 3.13.

Who would like to read all of the titles on this page?

Ask these questions:

1. What kind of book is this? (a fairy tale book)
2. How many stories are in the book? (8)
3. Would you check this book out if you were looking for the story of "Rapunzel"? (no)
4. Would you check this book out if you were looking for "Sleeping Beauty"? (yes)
5. Are the stories arranged in alphabetical order? (no)
6. In what order are the stories arranged? (in the order in which they appear in the book)
7. On which page does "Snow White" begin? (page 1)
8. On which page does it end? (page 11)
9. On which page does "Sleeping Beauty" end? (We don't know. The table of contents doesn't say.)
10. Which story starts on page 35? ("The Princess Who Never Laughed")

Collect the dittos.

Ask the students to take out their library books or textbooks.

Find the title page.

The table of contents is found after the title page. Find the table of contents.

Everyone's book may not have a table of contents.

If your book has a table of contents, raise your hand.

If only a few students find tables of contents, have them come to the front of the room to show their contents pages.

You may want to go quickly around the room to check each student.

I'm going to distribute a ditto that will give you an opportunity to work with a table of contents.

Distribute reproductions of Worksheet 3.14.

Who would like to read the titles?

Take out your pencils and go to work.

Correct the dittos with the students, or collect, correct, and return them later.

Table of Contents

Table of Contents

Worksheet 3.14 The Table of Contents

Table of Contents

Title	Page
Fun at the Zoo	1
The New Skates	12
Maybe I'll Be a Star	19
The Big Game	27
Bill's Red Bike	36
The Last Day of School	42

1. Which story starts on page 12? _____

2. On what page does "The Big Game" start? _____

3. On what page does it end? _____

4. How many stories are in the book? _____

5. Are the titles in ABC order? _____

6. Is the table of contents found in the front or the back of the book? _____

Lesson 31. The Table of Contents, Part II

OBJECTIVES

1. To introduce the variant term of table of contents: contents
2. To present two tables of contents for study
3. To check mastery with a follow-up ditto

MATERIALS

1. A nonfiction book containing a table of contents
2. A fiction book containing only one story
3. Back-to-back reproductions of Worksheets 3.15 and 3.16
4. A textbook for each student (It should have a table of contents and should be a different book from the one used in the previous lesson.)
5. Reproductions of Worksheet 3.17

LESSON

Hold up a nonfiction book containing a table of contents and a fiction book containing only one story. Read the titles aloud.

> Which book do you think has a table of contents? (the nonfiction book)

> I am going to distribute a ditto that shows two tables of contents.

Pass out the back-to-back reproductions of Worksheets 3.15 and 3.16.

> Look at Worksheet 3.15.

> Notice the heading: Contents. *Contents* and *table of contents* mean the same thing.

Ask the following questions:

1. Who wrote "The Yellow Cat"? (Jim Warner)
2. Which story did Fred Miller write? ("The Treehouse")
3. Which story starts on page 26? ("A Day at the Circus")
4. On what page does "Sing, Little Bird, Sing" begin? (page 10)
5. On what page does "New Shoes for Ann" end? (page 9)
6. What is the difference between a contents page and a table of contents page? (They are the same.)
7. Where is the contents page found in a book? (in the front)

Turn your dittos over to Worksheet 3.16.

Ask these questions:

1. Which story starts on page 42? ("Kitty Comes Home")
2. Who wrote "Roses for Mother"? (Sam Bell)
3. On what page does "Gone Fishing" begin? (page 36)
4. Which story did Dale Cannon write? ("Camping Out")
5. On what page does "The Long Way Home" end? (page 14)
6. Which story starts on page 25? ("An Afternoon in the Rain")

Collect the dittos.
Ask the students to take out a specific textbook.

Find the table of contents.

Ask questions similar to the ones asked above.

Put your books away.

I'm going to distribute a ditto.

Pass out reproductions of Worksheet 3.17.

Who would like to read the first title and author?

The second?

Continue until all of the titles and authors have been read.

Take out your pencils and do the paper.

Correct the dittos with the students, or collect, correct, and return them later.

Contents

Title	Author	Page
New Shoes for Ann	Rose Martin	1
Sing, Little Bird, Sing	Dick Green	10
The Yellow Cat	Jim Warner	18
A Day at the Circus	Susan Pitman	26
Ride a Gray Horse	Randy Smart	32
The Treehouse	Fred Miller	39

Contents

Title	Author	Page
The Long Way Home	Mary Wilson	1
Roses for Mother	Sam Bell	15
An Afternoon in the Rain	Roy Conway	25
Gone Fishing	Ann Hays	36
Kitty Comes Home	Ben Brown	42
Camping Out	Dale Cannon	50

Name _____ Date _____

Worksheet 3.17 The Table of Contents

Contents

Title	Author	Page
The Sad Giant	Ed Maxwell	1
The Last Bus Home	Pat Turner	8
Poems for Everyone	Brenda Wells	15
The Winner	Lee Sandman	24
A Dog for Joe	Gail Larson	33
The Boy Who Wasn't Afraid	Dave Hunt	41

1. Which story begins on page 33? _____

2. On what page does "The Winner" begin? _____

3. Who wrote "The Sad Giant"? _____

4. On what page does "The Last Bus Home" end? _____

5. Did Brenda Wells write a story or poems? _____
   (Don't answer yes or no. Answer story or poems.)

6. Which story did Dave Hunt write? _____

_____

Lesson 32. The Glossary

OBJECTIVES

1. To introduce glossaries
2. To present two glossaries for examination
3. To guide a search for glossaries in the students' library books and textbooks
4. To give practice in the use of a textbook glossary

MATERIALS

1. A book with a glossary for demonstration (Geography books often have glossaries.)
2. Back-to-back ditto reproductions of Worksheets 3.18 and 3.19
3. Any available library books and textbooks

LESSON

Open a book to its glossary and hold it up.

> Some books have glossaries. A *glossary* is a list of the special or difficult words found in a book. The glossary gives the meaning and sometimes the pronunciation of these words. It's a little dictionary for the particular book in which it's found.

Inform the students that you're going to distribute a ditto. Pass out reproductions of the glossaries on Worksheets 3.18 and 3.19.

> Look at the glossary on Worksheet 3.18.
>
> What is a glossary? (A glossary is a small dictionary. It gives the meaning and sometimes the pronunciation of the special or difficult words of a particular book.)
>
> The special words, for which the definitions are given, are called *entry words*.
>
> Point to the entry word at the top of the page.
>
> Did you point to the word *break*?
>
> What is the second entry word? (bronco)
>
> The third? (cantle)
>
> Are the entry words in a glossary arranged in alphabetical order? (yes)
>
> Where is a glossary found? (in the back of a book)

Call on students to read the meanings of the following entry words: chaps, gaucho, and rodeo.

Look at the glossary on Worksheet 3.19 on the other side of your ditto.

How is this glossary different from the one we just examined? (It includes the pronunciation of words.)

What is the meaning of *caribou?*

What is the pronunciation of the word spelled k-a-y-a-k?

What is the meaning of *tundra?*

What is the pronunciation of the word spelled u-l-u?

Collect the dittos.

Tell the students to take all of their library books out of their desks. Ask them to examine their books to see if any of them have glossaries. If they do have glossaries, the students are to raise their hands.

If there are just a few students with their hands up, call on them, one at a time, to give the titles of their books and to hold their books open to the glossaries.

Call attention to the types of books in which the students found glossaries.

If one of the textbooks has a glossary, have all of the students find the glossary in their copy of that textbook. Read words from the textbook glossary and have students find them. Call on students to read the definitions.

What is a glossary? (A glossary is a small dictionary. It gives the meaning and sometimes the pronunciation of the special or difficult words of a particular book.)

Tell the students to put their books away.

Glossary

break (a horse)—tame

bronco—an unbroken or imperfectly broken range horse

cantle—back of the saddle

chaps—leather leggings worn over regular pants as leg protectors

chuck wagon—covered wagon which carries food during a trail drive

cowboy—worker who rides horseback much of the time while herding and tending cattle

cowhand—cowboy who is a hired hand, or a worker who tends cows

cowpoke—cowboy

cowpuncher—cowboy

flank—right side

gaucho—a cowboy or herdsman of the pampas, usually of mixed Spanish and Indian descent

honda—the end of the lariat which is knotted to form a small eye

line camps—small outposts

reata—rope

rodeo—competition to determine best rider, roper, and broncobuster

vaqueros—Mexican cowboys

Glossary

caribou—(kăr′ ĭ bo͞o), North American reindeer

harpoon—(här pün′), spear with a rope tied to it

igloo—(ig′ lü), Eskimo dome-like hut, often made of snow

kayak—(kī′ ak), an Eskimo canoe

snow knife—(snō′ nīf), a long, straight knife made of bone

soapstone—(sōp′ stōn′), soft rock from which Eskimos make lamps and cooking pots

sod—(sod), ground covered with grass

tundra—(tun′ drə), treeless plain that is characteristic of arctic and subarctic regions

ulu—(o͞o′ lo͞o), an Eskimo woman's knife

umiak—(o͞o′ mĭ ăk), an open Eskimo boat about 50 feet long and 8 feet wide

Lesson 33. The Index, Part I

OBJECTIVES

1. To introduce indexes
2. To present two indexes for study
3. To teach the students how to read page numbers

MATERIALS

1. A chalkboard, chalk, and eraser
2. Back-to-back reproductions of Worksheets 3.20 and 3.21

PREPARATION

Put these numbers on the chalkboard in three lines, as given here.

86–9, 101–6, 109

6, 16, 32, 64

9–11, 64–9, 100–8

LESSON

Suppose you found a 300-page book at the library on pets. If you were only interested in reading about cats, would you have to read all 300 pages to find what you wanted? No. You would turn to the back of the book to the index. The index is an alphabetical list of all the subjects in a book. It gives the page numbers on which each subject is found. In the index you would find the page numbers for cats. You would then turn to those pages and read.

The index is very useful. It tells you exactly which pages have the information you are seeking.

I'm going to pass out a double-sided ditto with examples of two indexes.

Distribute reproductions of Worksheets 3.20 and 3.21.

Look at the index on Worksheet 3.20.

See the words farthest to the left. Those are called *entry words*—they're the main subjects. Notice that they are arranged alphabetically. Follow with your finger as I read them: cats, dogs, goldfish, mice, rabbits. There are five subjects—five entry words.

Now find "cats." Do you see some words under "cats" that are indented three spaces? Follow with your finger while I read them: choosing, feeding, kinds, training. These are subdivisions of the subject "cats."

Let's say you want to read about training cats. You would find "cats" in the index. Then you would look at the subdivisions, which are in alphabetical order. Look down the list until you come to "training."

On which pages will you find information about training cats? (pages 57–62)

That's right. Pages 57 *through* 62.

The hyphen means through. Let's all count on our fingers and see how many pages there are from page 57 through page 62. Count: 57, 58, 59, 60, 61, 62. We counted six pages. There are six pages on training cats.

Look again at the entry word "cats." Next to the entry word we see 44–62. That means that everything about cats can be found on pages 44 through 62. However, you may not be interested in reading all about cats. You may just be interested in reading about feeding cats.

On which pages would you find information about feeding cats? (pages 52–56)

Be sure that the students say *through* when there is a hyphen.

How many pages are about feeding cats? Count silently on your fingers. (5 pages)

On which pages can you find all the information there is about goldfish? (pages 63–72)

Which pages are about feeding goldfish? (pages 67–68)

Continue asking similar questions, if needed.

Turn the ditto over to Worksheet 3.21. This is the first part of another index.

On which page would you find information about John Adams? (page 123)

Was he listed under his first or last name? (last name)

On which page would you find information about homes? (page 72)

Is this index in alphabetical order? (yes)

On which pages would you find information about books and libraries? (pages 125, 163–6)

Be sure the student reads the pages like this: 125 *and* 163 *through* 166.

How many pages would that be? Count on your fingers. 125 is one page. Then we have 163, 164, 165, 166. (5 pages)

On which pages would we find information about fishing? (pages 61–3, 115–19, 169)

Be sure the student reads this 61 *through* 63 *and* 115 *through* 119 *and* 169.

Under "fishing" you see a cross reference: *see also* shipbuilding. That means if you have not found enough information under fishing, you can also look under shipbuilding, which may have some related information that you can use.

On which pages would you find information about candles? (pages 12, 15, 18, 37)

There are two ways to read these numbers. You could say 12, *and* 15 *and* 18 *and* 37. A comma means "and." However, it's a little boring to hear so many "ands." A better way to read the numbers would be to pause slightly for each comma.

Read the numbers for the students using slight pauses instead of "ands." (12, 15, 18, 37)

I have put some page numbers on the board. Who wants to read the first line?

Be sure the student reads this precisely: 86 *through* 89 *and* 101 *through* 106, *and* 109. Pauses can be substituted for "ands."

Who wants to read the second line?

Be sure the student uses slight pauses between the numbers instead of saying "and" each time.

Who wants to read the last line?

This should be read like this: 9 *through* 11 *and* 64 *through* 69 *and* 100 *through* 108.

Pauses may be used instead of "ands."

You did a good job.

Worksheet 3.20 The Index

Index

Worksheet 3.21 The Index

Index

Adams, John 123
almanacs 98
books and libraries 125, 163–6
candles 12, 15, 18, 37
fishing 61–3, 115–19, 169
   see also shipbuilding
homes 72

Lesson 34. The Index, Part II

OBJECTIVES

1. To review indexes
2. To review reading page numbers
3. To present an index for study
4. To give practice in the use of a textbook index
5. To check mastery with a follow-up ditto

MATERIALS

1. A chalkboard, chalk, and eraser
2. Reproductions of Worksheet 3.22
3. Reproductions of Worksheet 3.23 (The two reproductions should *not* be put back to back.)
4. Any textbooks that have indexes

PREPARATIONS

1. Put the following pages on the board:

    43, 84–8, 100–3
    101–8, 64, 92–6
    28, 33–7, 200–7

2. Look through your classroom textbooks. Note the ones whose indexes would be suitable for using with this lesson.

LESSON

Who remembers what an index is? (a list of the subjects in a book and the page numbers where the subjects are found)

Are indexes arranged in alphabetical order? (yes)

Where is an index located in a book? (in the back)

Who can explain how an index can be helpful to you? (It tells you on which page you can find what you're looking for.)

I've put some index page numbers on the board. Who can read the first line? (43 *and* 84 *through* 88 *and* 100 *through* 103)

The second line? (101 *through* 108 *and* 64 *and* 92 *through* 96)

The third line? (28 *and* 33 *through* 37 *and* 200 *through* 207)

I'm going to pass out an index ditto, which we will look at together.

Distribute reproductions of Worksheet 3.22.

Look at the top of the index. Under the word *index,* it reads: "Explanation of abbreviations used in this Index." On the next line it says that the letter "p" will be used to mean pictures and "m" will be used to mean maps.

See how the page is divided into three columns.

Hold up the index and designate the three columns.

Look at the first column. Do you see how the entry words—the subjects—are in dark black letters?

Write this on the board: candles.

On which pages would you find written information about candles? (pages 38–43)

On which pages would you find pictures of candles? (pages 38, 39, 41–43)

Let's look at these pages closely.

Write the pages on the board: 38–43; *p* 38, 39, 41–43.

The first pages, 38–43, have written information.

See the semicolon.

Point to the semicolon.

The semicolon means stop. The pages before the semicolon are the only pages with written information.

On the right of the semicolon we see the letter "p," which means pictures. We don't see any stop sign so that means all the pages after "p" have pictures.

Write this on the board: Middle Colonies.

Find "Middle Colonies" in the index.

The letter "m" means map.

On which page is there a map? (page 8)

Circulate and see that students are locating the pages.

Find "schools."

See the subdivisions: colleges, dame schools, plantation, and public schools.

On which pages would you find information about public schools? (pages 79–81)

On which page would you find a picture of a public school? (page 80)

Write this on the board: dress.

Find "dress."

Did you find a page number? (no)

You found a cross reference. You were told to look under clothing. There's nothing wrong with looking under the word *dress*. The author decided to use the word *clothing* instead, so the index is telling you to look there.

Find "clothing" as you were directed to do.

Under "clothing" look at the subdivision "in the Middle Colonies."

Which pages have pictures? (pages 63, 64)

Which pages have written information? (pages 63–65)

If you have a textbook with a good index, tell your students to take the book out. Ask them to find the index. Then ask questions similar to the ones above.

I'm going to distribute a ditto for you to do. It's about the index. Look at the index I gave you to find the answers for this ditto.

Take out your pencils and get ready.

Distribute reproductions of Worksheet 3.23.
Check the papers with the students, or collect, correct, and return them later.

INDEX

Explanation of abbreviations used in this Index:

p — pictures   *m* — maps

© 1990 by Arden Druce

From *Colonial America*. Reprinted courtesy of Gateway Press, Inc./Fideler Books

Worksheet 3.23 The Index

Look at the index that your teacher gave to you on Worksheet 3.22. Find the answers to these questions:

1. On which pages will you find written information about churches? _____

   _____

2. On which pages will you find pictures of churches? _____

   _____

3. Which pages give written information about earning a living? _____

   _____

4. Which pages give written information about fishing? _____

   _____

5. On which pages will you find pictures of newspapers? _____

   _____

6. Which page gives written information about a shoemaker? _____

   _____

7. Which page has a picture of a wigmaker? _____

   _____

8. If you look under education, you will be told to look under _____

   _____ instead.

9. On which page will you find written information about Swedish homes? _____

   _____

10. Which pages will give you written information about the spinning wheels that are used to spin

    wool? _____

Lesson 35. Written Book Reports

OBJECTIVE

To teach students how to make a written book report

MATERIALS

1. Make reproductions of a book report form (Select from Worksheets 3.24, 3.25, and 3.26.)
2. A fiction book for each student

LESSON

> Sometimes after reading a book you share what you've read. You might share it in one of several ways. You might tell a friend about it. You might give an oral book report in front of the class. An oral book report means a book report given through speech. Or you might share your book by making a written book report.
>
> I would like each of you to select a book for a written report. Choose a fiction book that is similar in difficulty to your reading textbook. Bring the book to me for my approval. You must have my approval. Read the entire book. You can't report on a book unless you've read all of it.
>
> I'm going to distribute a report form.

After passing out the form, read through it and discuss the different parts.

> When you are reading your book, you'll want to keep this form in mind. You can be thinking of what information you'll need to complete your report.

After the reports are finished, you may want to put them in a folder and make them available for student reading. If you plan to do this, tell the students now to increase their motivation. You may want to title the folder "Book Reviews."

> Your reports will be due on _____.
>
> Write your name on the form and put it in your desk.

Worksheet 3.24 Book Report

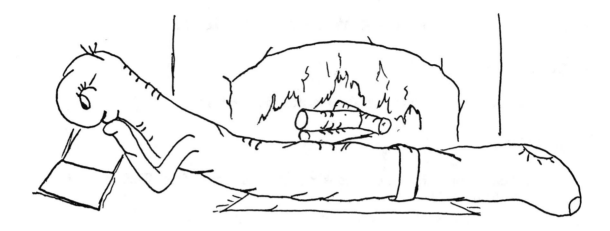

Title _____

Author _____

What the story is about.

_____

_____

_____

_____

_____

_____

_____

_____

Rating
(circle one)

poor   fair   good   excellent

Write the name of one friend who would like to read this book.

_____

Name _____ **Date** _____

Worksheet 3.25 Book Report

Title _____

Author _____

Explain the story briefly _____

_____

_____

_____

_____

_____

_____

_____

Why did you choose this book? _____

_____

_____

_____

_____

Would you recommend this book to another reader? _____

Why or why not? _____

_____

_____

_____

_____

Name _____ **Date** _____

Worksheet 3.26 Book Report

Title _____

Author _____

Main Characters _____

_____

_____

_____

_____

Summary _____

_____

_____

_____

_____

_____

_____

_____

Favorite Part _____

_____

_____

_____

_____

Rating (circle one)   poor   fair   good   excellent

Why did you give the book the rating that you did?

_____

_____

_____

Lesson 36. Oral Book Reports

OBJECTIVES

1. To teach students how to give oral book reports
2. To teach students to be courteous listeners

MATERIALS

1. A chalkboard, chalk, and eraser
2. Reproductions of Worksheet 3.27
3. A sign-up schedule posted on the bulletin board (See "Preparations" section below.)

PREPARATIONS

1. If you have a library, schedule a visit for the day you present this lesson.
2. Put the following example of your book report schedule on the board. Change the dates to those you will be using.

    Oct. 1 _____   _____   _____
    Oct. 2 _____   _____   _____
    Oct. 3 _____   _____   _____

LESSON

Sometimes you share a book you've read with another person. What you're really doing is introducing the person to a new book. If you shared a book, not with just one person, but with a whole class, think of how many people you'd be introducing your book to.

When students stand in front of a class and tell about a book they've read, we say they're giving a book report. There are two kinds of book reports. There are written book reports and oral book reports. An oral book report is a report you give through speech.

I would like to give each one of you an opportunity to give an oral book report. I have posted a schedule on the bulletin board. The schedule looks like this.

Point to the board.

By each date there are spaces for three students' names. There are enough dates and spaces on the schedule so that everyone can sign up.

If you sign up to give your report on October 6, then you must be ready by that date.

You must report on a book that is similar in difficulty to your reading textbook. You may select either fiction or nonfiction. Bring the book that you select to me for my approval. You must have my approval. Read the entire book. You can't report on a book unless you've read all of it.

First, select your book. Second, get my approval. Third, read your book. And last of all, prepare your report. You should be thoroughly prepared before giving your report. You should have thought out everything you are going to say, and you should have thought out the order in which you are going to say everything.

I'm going to pass out a ditto that gives instructions on how to prepare your report.

Distribute ditto reproductions of Worksheet 3.27.

Read the page together and discuss it.

If you want your students to remember the rules on the bottom half of the ditto, you might try this. Have a student take a book to the front of the room. As you read the rules one by one, the student should act them out. Instead of giving a report, have the student read a short paragraph for this demonstration.

Repeat the procedure with another student. However, this time the student should do the opposite of what the rules call for. The student should demonstrate what *not* to do.

We will begin our oral book reports in one week. That will give you time to read a book and get prepared. Sign up on the schedule today or tomorrow.

Write your name on your oral book report ditto and put it in your desk for future use.

If you have a library, take your students for a visit and help them select their books.

FOLLOW-UP

On the day that the oral reports start, precede the first report with the following instructions about listening and courtesy.

When a student is giving an oral report, he or she is not the only one who is learning. Everyone in the room is learning. The listeners are learning to be courteous. Eventually the listeners will be speakers and they will want everyone to listen politely to them.

By listening and watching the speakers carefully, the audience can learn which techniques are most effective in reporting. In other words, they can learn what to do and what not to do.

If you notice something especially good about a report, why don't you tell the reporter when you have a chance. You'd like someone to tell you when you do something especially effective. Other people like praise, too.

In praising people, be sincere. *Sincere* means truthful. Don't say something if you don't mean it.

Worksheet 3.27 Oral Book Reports

Include these things in your book report:

1. Show the book, if possible.

2. Give the title and author.

3. If the illustrations are an important part of the book, give the illustrator's name.

4. Tell, in a few sentences, what the book is about.

5. Tell about an especially interesting part, or read a short part aloud. (Teacher's choice)

6. Tell just enough to make the listeners want to know more. Never give away the surprises in the book.

7. Show some of the pictures, if there are any of interest.

8. Tell why you think your listeners would like the book.

9. Give your opinion of the book.

When giving your book report, do these things:

1. Stand up tall, with your hands at your side.

2. Face the class.

3. Don't lean against anything.

4. Pause until everybody is looking before you start to speak.

5. Speak clearly and project your voice so that the last person in the room can hear.

6. Finish the report before starting to walk away.

UNIT 4

FOURTH GRADE

What to Teach in Fourth Grade

SUGGESTIONS

1. Before your first trip to the library, refer to Appendix A, "How to Conduct Library Visits."
2. Lessons, reproducible forms, and guidelines for book reports are found in Unit 3. Written book report forms are found in Lesson 35; Oral book reports are discussed in Lesson 36. Use these materials intermittently whenever the need arises.
3. You may want to use a green (go) marker and a red (stop) marker to designate the pages you need to teach.

LESSONS

Begin by teaching Lesson 20 ("Book Care and Library Behavior") and Lesson 21 ("Appreciating Books") from Unit 3. These lessons need to be retaught each year.

If you know that your students haven't received instruction in library skills, teach Lessons 22A through 36, lessons from Unit 3. Then teach Lessons 37 through 53 in this unit. These lessons will bring the students up to grade level plus carry them through the lessons for fourth grade.

If you don't know whether your students have had instruction in library skills or if you have reason to believe that they have had instruction, use Pretest 1 in Appendix B to determine subject mastery.

If your students do poorly on the pretest, assume either that they have not had library instruction or that they need to have a complete reteaching of previous lessons. For bringing the students up to beginning fourth grade level, teach Lessons 22A through 36. Thereafter, to cover fourth grade skills, teach the lessons in this unit.

If your students do well on the pretest except for a couple of items, teach only the lessons related to those specific items to bring the students up to grade level. (The pretest answer page specifies the lesson in which each item was introduced.) After bringing the class up to grade level, teach the lessons in this unit, which cover fourth grade skills.

If your students do well on the pretest, they are up to grade level. To cover fourth grade skills, teach the lessons in this unit.

Lesson 37. Fiction, Part I

OBJECTIVES

1. To introduce fiction
2. To teach how fiction is arranged in a library
3. To teach the students how to read book spines
4. To check mastery with a ditto follow-up

MATERIALS

1. Six fiction books (Familiar titles such as *Charlotte's Web, The Wizard of Oz, The Tough Winter, Encyclopedia Brown Takes the Case, Miss Pickerell and the Blue Whale,* and *The Borrowers Afloat* would be appropriate. Choose books that are easily identified as fiction.)
2. Three nonfiction books (Books about snakes, spiders, and airplanes would be good choices. Choose books that are easily identified as nonfiction.)
3. An easy book and a picture book
4. Back-to-back reproductions of Worksheets 4.1 and 4.2

PREPARATION

Draw four book spines on the board. Make them 18 inches tall by 9 inches wide, or larger. Letter them like the examples below.

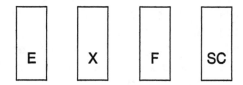

LESSON

Hold up a fiction book. Read the title.

This book is not true; it's made up. It's fiction.

Hold up a second fiction book. Read the title.

This book is fiction, too. It's not true.

Hold up a third fiction book. Read the title.

This book is made up; it's not true. It's fiction.

I'm going to hold up several books. If I hold up a fiction book, raise your hand. If I hold up a true book, don't raise your hand.

Remember, fiction is not true; it's made up.

Hold up some fiction and nonfiction books, one at a time. The students should respond by raising their hands when you hold up a fiction book.

Ask the class which of the following titles are fiction:

1. *Island Mystery* (F)
2. *California Today*
3. *How to Repair Your Bike*
4. *Peter Rabbit* (F)
5. *Abraham Lincoln*
6. *Butterflies*
7. *The Muppets Go Camping* (F)
8. *Return of the Jedi* (F)
9. *How They Built the Statue of Liberty*
10. *The Story of Superman* (F)

You can't always tell whether a book is fiction by its title, but many times you can.

Some children's libraries divide fiction into two groups: easy-to-read fiction and fiction that is harder to read. Other libraries divide children's fiction into three or four groups: easy-to-read fiction, fiction that is harder to read, picture books, and story collections.

Easy books is the usual term for easy-to-read fiction. Easy books have an "E" on their spines.

Hold up an easy book and point to the spine. (If needed, see the glossary for a picture of a spine.)

This is the spine of a book.

I have drawn four spines on the board.

Point to the first spine.

"E" on the spine means easy.

A picture book is a book in which the pictures are large and are an important part of the book.

Introduce a picture book. Read its title. Show several of its pictures.

Some libraries shelve picture books with easy fiction. They put an "E" on the spines of picture books.

Point to the first spine on the board.

Other libraries put picture books all by themselves. An "X" is put on their spines.

Point to the second spine.

Fiction that is harder to read is just called *fiction.*

Point to the third spine.

"F" means fiction.

Short stories are shelved with fiction in some libraries. In other libraries they are shelved separately. When short stories are shelved separately, they are referred to as the *story collection,* and an "SC" is put on their spines.

Point to the fourth spine.

Easy books and fiction are shelved separately.

If you are in the library, point out the location of the different kinds of fiction and explain how your library shelves each kind.

Today we will discuss two kinds of fiction: easy books and fiction.

I'm going to pass out a ditto that shows how easy books and fiction are arranged on library shelves.

Distribute the back-to-back reproductions of Worksheets 4.1 and 4.2.

Look at the top half of Worksheet 4.1.

Each of the books at the top of the page has an "E" on it.

Who can tell me what the "E" stands for? (Easy, easy books, easy-to-read, or easy-to-read fiction would all be acceptable. In some libraries picture books are classified as easy books. An "E" on a picture book's spine would mean picture books are being shelved in the easy section.)

Study the arrangement of the books.

Are the books arranged by author or title? (author)

What is the title of the first easy book? (*The Friendly Book*)

Who is the author? (Brown)

What do the letters under "E" stand for? (They are the first letters of the author's last name.)

Continue. Ask the students to identify the title, author, and author's letters for each of the four remaining easy books.

Look at the bottom half of the ditto.

What does "F" stand for? (fiction)

What does "Fic" stand for? (fiction)

The third book doesn't have "F" or "Fic" on its spine. It only has three letters of the author's last name.

What kind of book is it? (fiction)

Fiction can be labeled with "F," "Fic," or just with one, two, or three letters of the author's last name.

Study the arrangement of the fiction books.

Are the books arranged by author or title? (author)

What is the title of the first book? (*Ramona the Pest*)

Who is the author? (Cleary)

Look at the five fiction spines. What are the letters at the bottom edge? (They are the first letters of the authors' last names.)

Ask the students to identify the title, author, and author's letters for each of the four remaining fiction books.

Easy and fiction books are both arranged by the authors' last names.

If you haven't told your students how your library divides fiction, tell them now. Does your library have only two sections of fiction: easy books and fiction? If so, picture books are shelved with easy books and short stories are shelved with fiction. If either picture books or short stories are shelved separately, tell your class.

Instruct the students to turn over their dittos. After explaining the paper, tell the students to put their names at the top of the page and to start working.

SUGGESTIONS

1. If you have time, you may want to make some easy and/or fiction spines for use on the flannel board.

    Cut tagboard into 18 by 9 inch spines. Paste either sandpaper or felt strips on the back.

    Alternative: Copy the spines on the board.

2. During a review, place an unalphabetized set of spines on the flannel board. Call on someone to come to the front of the room and put the spines in order. Discuss how the student arrived at his or her arrangement.

    Place another set of spines on the flannel board for a second student to put in order.

    Students like this activity and it is very effective.

    Here are some spines appropriate for this lesson.

    Set 1:

Amelia Bedelia Parish E Par	The Biggest Bear Ward E War	The Cat in the Hat Seuss E Seu

    Set 2:

Crow Boy Yashima E Yas	The Dragon and the Mouse Timm E Tim	The Five Chinese Brothers Bishop E Bis

    An alternative or supplementary approach is to make two sets of sentence strips for the students to arrange on the flannel board. Alternative: Copy the strips on the board. Here are some sentence strips appropriate for this lesson.

    Set 1:

Balian	Humbug Rabbit

Ets	Gilberto and the Wind

Zion	Harry the Dirty Dog

Set 2:

Green	Hole in the Dike

Hoff	Henrietta, Circus Star

Seuss	Green Eggs and Ham

3. If you have learning centers in your room or library, you may want to use this idea. Get five or six fiction or easy books, and put them on a learning center table. Let one student at a time visit the center, put the books in correct order, and then check his or her own work from an answer card. When finished, the student should disarrange the books so that they will be ready for the next person. The books must all be the same kind—either all easy or all fiction.

Worksheet 4.1 Fiction Arrangement

Easy Books

The Friendly Book	Are You My Mother?	The Fat Cat	Mouse Tales	Peter Rabbit
Brown	Eastman	Kent	Lobel	Potter
E Bro	E Eas	E Ken	E Lob	E Pot

Fiction

Ramona the Pest	Black Stallion	"B" Is for Betsy	Mary Poppins	Little House on the Prairie
Cleary	Farley	Haywood	Travers	Wilder
F Cle	Fic Far	Hay	F Tr	Fic Wil

Name _____   **Date** _____

Worksheet 4.2 Arranging Fiction Books

Fiction is arranged in alphabetical order by the authors' last names.

Put these books in order by writing the names of the authors in order on the lines below.

Caddie Woodlawn	A Chair for My Mother	Henry Reed, Inc.	Jane, Wishing	Homer Price
Brink	Williams	Robertson	Tobias	McCloskey
F Bri	Fic Wil	F Rob	Tob	F McC

1. _____

2. _____

3. _____

4. _____

5. _____

Lesson 38. Fiction, Part II

OBJECTIVES

1. To review easy books and fiction
2. To teach more about short story collections
3. To introduce the use of authors' first names
4. To check mastery with a ditto follow-up

MATERIALS

1. Optional: A book that has several stories (Select a book from the section where short stories are shelved in your library: from the short story collection or from fiction. Do not select a fairy tale book. Fairy tales are classified as nonfiction.)
2. A chalkboard, chalk, and eraser
3. Back-to-back reproductions of Worksheets 4.3 and 4.4

LESSON

You've learned a number of things about fiction. Today you're going to learn some more. Let's start by finding out what you remember from our last lesson.

Ask these questions:

1. What is fiction? (books or stories that are made up, not true, imaginary)
2. How is fiction arranged on library shelves? (by the authors' last names)
3. Into which four groups may fiction be divided? (easy, picture books, fiction, story collection)

Write the following on the board, and then point to each item as you ask its meaning: Fic   F   E   X   SC.

What does "Fic" mean? "F"? "E"? "X"? "SC"? (fiction, fiction, easy, picture book, story collection)

Write the following on the board: Smi.

If you saw this on a book's spine, what would you know about the book? (It's fiction and the author's last name starts with "Smi.")

We talked about easy books and fiction in detail during our last lesson. Today we're going to learn about short story collections.

Books that contain short stories are shelved either in fiction or in a special section called the *story collection*. If they are shelved separately, "SC" for story collection is put on their spines.

Short story collections are arranged by the authors' last names.

If you have a book with several short stories, show it to the students. Read the titles of some of the stories.

There are four kinds of fiction: easy, picture books, fiction, and collections of stories. They are all arranged by the authors' last names.

Sometimes there are two authors with the same last name. In that case, the authors' first names are considered.

Write Ann Smith on the board. Under it write Betty Smith.

Ann Smith's book would be shelved before Betty Smith's book.

Fiction may be divided into four groups: easy, picture books, fiction, and story collections. Our library divides fiction into _____ groups: _____.

Inform the class that you are going to pass out a ditto that will give them some practice in putting fiction books in order. Pass out the back-to-back reproductions of Worksheets 4.3 and 4.4.

Worksheet 4.3 Arranging Fiction Books

These books are not in order. Put them in order on the spines below. Remember, fiction is arranged by the authors' last names.

Rufus M.	Winter Danger	Superfudge	Star Wars	Ben and Me
Estes	Steele	Blume	Weinberg	Lawson
Fic Est	F Ste	Fic Blu	Fic Wei	Law

Worksheet 4.4 Arranging Easy Books

These books are not in order. Put them in order on the spines below. Remember, easy books are arranged by the authors' last names.

Tale of a Black Cat	When I Was Young in the Mountains	Sylvester and the Magic Pebble	Danny and the Dinosaur	Petunia
Withers	Rylant	Steig	Hoff	Duvoisin
E Wit	E Ryl	E Ste	E Hof	E Duv

Lesson 39. Fiction, Part III

OBJECTIVES

1. To review fiction
2. To introduce the use of titles in arranging fiction
3. To explain that the words *a, an,* and *the* are disregarded as first words in titles
4. To check mastery with a ditto follow-up

MATERIALS

1. A chalkboard, chalk, and eraser
2. Back-to-back reproductions of Worksheets 4.5 and 4.6

PREPARATIONS

1. Copy these spines on the board.

Betsy and Billy	Eddie and Gardenia	Little Eddie
Haywood	Haywood	Haywood
F Hay	F Hay	F Hay

2. Make a second set of spines similar to the set above for the following three books by Estes: *Witch Family, Pinky Pye,* and *Middle Moffat.*

3. If you would like to have a third set, use these three titles by Cleary: *Ramona Forever, Socks,* and *Beezus and Ramona.*

   Put the preceding titles on the board in the order in which they are given. The titles in Set 1, which are in order, are for presenting correct arrangement. The titles in the second and third sets are not in the correct order. They are to be numbered in the correct order by students.

4. Copy the following authors and titles on the board. Don't copy the answers in parentheses.

Set 1	Brown	*The Last Prize*	(3)
	Brown	*A Chance to Win*	(2)
	Brown	*An Afternoon to Remember*	(1)

Set 2	Johnson	*The Way Home*	(3)
	Johnson	*A Day at the Beach*	(2)
	Johnson	*An Adventure*	(1)
Set 3	Miller	*Come Rain or Shine*	(2)
	Miller	*An Umbrella for Me*	(3)
	Miller	*The Brightest Star*	(1)

LESSON

You've learned a great deal about fiction. Let's see what you remember.

Ask these questions:

1. What is fiction? (made-up books *or* books that aren't true)
2. What are the four kinds of fiction? (easy, picture books, fiction, story collection)
3. How are they arranged on library shelves? (by the authors' last names)
4. How would you decide whose book to shelve first if two authors had the same last name? (Decide between the two by their first names.)
5. (Write these on the board: Fic F E X SC)
   What does each of these mean? (fiction, fiction, easy, picture book, story collection)

Arrange fiction books by author. If an author has written more than one book, arrange the books secondarily by their titles.

Point to the Haywood spines on the board.

Look at these spines.

Notice that Haywood is the author of all three of these books. The books are already arranged by author. Secondarily, which means second, the books are arranged by title. Looking at the titles we can see that *Betsy and Billy* comes first. *Eddie and Gardenia* comes second. *Little Eddie* is third.

If you have put the second and third sets of spines on the board, explain that they are not in order.
Call on someone to number the second set in order.
Discuss how the student arrived at the numbering.
Call on someone to number the third set in order.
Discuss how the student arrived at the numbering.

Most book titles start with either the words *a, an, or the*. For that reason these three words are disregarded as first words in a title. They are considered only if they are in any position other than first.

Look at the authors and titles on the board.

Who can number the first set in order? (3, 2, 1)

Tell the student who does the example to cross out any words he or she isn't going to use.

After the student has numbered the titles, discuss how he or she arrived at the numbering.

Who can number the second set in order? (3, 2, 1)

After the student has numbered the titles, discuss how he or she arrived at the numbers.

Who can number the third set in order? (2, 3, 1)

I'm going to distribute a double-sided ditto for you to do.

Pass out the back-to-back reproductions of Worksheets 4.5 and 4.6.

Correct the papers together, discussing how the students should have arrived at the correct order.

Worksheet 4.5 Arranging Fiction Books

These books are not in order. Put them in order on the spines below. Remember, fiction is arranged by the authors' last names. If an author has written more than one book, arrange the books by title secondarily.

Dear Mr. Henshaw	Mr. Revere and I	Henry and Ribsy	Paddington Bear	Ben and Me
Cleary	Lawson	Cleary	Bond	Lawson
F Cle	Fic Law	Cle	Fic Bon	F Law

Worksheet 4.6 Arranging Easy Books

These books are not in order. Copy them in order on the spines below. Remember, easy books are arranged first by the authors' last names. If an author has written more than one book, arrange the books by title secondarily. Disregard the words *a, an,* and *the* as first words of titles when alphabetizing.

Ox-Cart Man	Owl at Home	The Story About Ping	An Eagle Returns	Back Home
Hall	Lobel	Flack	Brown	Brown
E Hal	E Lob	E Fla	E Bro	E Bro

Lesson 40. Fiction Review

OBJECTIVES

1. To review fiction
2. To check mastery with a ditto follow-up

MATERIALS

1. A chalkboard, chalk, and eraser
2. Back-to-back reproductions of Worksheets 4.7 and 4.8

PREPARATION

Put the following sets on the board at a height students can reach. (Don't copy the answers in parentheses.)

Set 1	Johnson	*The New Teacher*	(3)
	Brown	*Riding High*	(1)
	Dawson	*Wait for Me*	(2)
Set 2	Adams, Dan	*Alice's Friend*	(2)
	Brown, Betty	*The Surprise*	(3)
	Adams, Ann	*Win or Lose*	(1)
Set 3	Wells	*A Zoo for Joe*	(3)
	Bates	*Wishing on a Star*	(1)
	Wells	*The Last One Home*	(2)

LESSON

You've learned a lot about fiction. Let's see what you remember.

Ask these questions:

1. What is fiction? (made-up books *or* stories)
2. Can you name one or more of the four groups into which fiction may be divided? (easy, picture books, fiction, story collection)
3. How is fiction arranged on the shelf? (by the authors' last names)
4. How do you arrange two fiction books by authors who have the same last name? (Use the authors' first names to decide which comes first.)
5. If an author has written several books, how do you decide which to put first? (Put them by title secondarily.)

6. Which words do we throw away or disregard as first words in a title? (a, an, the)

7. Write these on the board: E   X   F   Fic   SC   What do these mean? (easy book, picture book, fiction, fiction, story collection)

I've put some authors and titles on the board.

Who would like to number the first set in order?

After a student has numbered the first set, discuss the fact that he or she had to look only at the authors' names and alphabetize them.

Notice that the second set has some names that have commas.

To explain what the commas mean, I'll put an example on the board using one of your names.

Select one of the students' names, e.g., Susie Jones.

This is the way (Susie) writes her name. When I put (Susie's) name in my roll book, I write her last name first.

Write on the board: (Jones, Susie)

Notice that I put a comma after her last name. That comma is a signal—warning that (Susie's) last name is first.

(Susie's) name is not (Jones Susie); it's (Susie Jones).

Whenever a last name is put first, a comma is always used to warn people of that fact.

Put a couple more of your students' names on the board with the last names first.

What do the commas in these names mean? (The last names have been written first.)

When reading a name that has been written with the last name first, read it like the student would say it if you asked his or her name. In other words, read the first name first.

Call on a student to read the first name on the board.
Call on another student to read the second name.

Let's look back at the authors and titles on the board.

Who would like to number the second set in order?

After a student has numbered the second set in order, discuss the fact that since the two authors had the same last name, the authors' first names had to be considered.

Who would like to number the third set in order?

After a student has numbered the third set in order, discuss the fact that Wells wrote two of the books. Explain that to decide which of the two books had to be put first, one had to alphabetize them by title.

> I'm going to distribute a double-sided ditto. Let's see how much you've learned about fiction.

Pass out the ditto.

Worksheet 4.7 Fiction Quiz

Answer the following questions:

1. Is fiction true or not true?

   _____

2. Is fiction arranged by the author's first or last name?

   _____

3. If you were putting books in order by the following two authors, which would come first: Steven Gray or Janet Gray?

   _____

4. If an author has written several fiction books, should the books be arranged among themselves by title or by subject?

   _____

5. Which three of these words—*a, of, an, it, the, in*—are disregarded as first words in a title?

   _____

Name _____   Date _____

Worksheet 4.8 Arranging Fiction Books

These books are not in order. Put them in order on the spines below.

A Smile for Me	Ride the Wind	Lost in the Woods	Going Home	The New Car
Bond	Turner	Long	Bond	Green
F Bon	F Tur	Fic Lon	Bon	Fic Gre

Lesson 41. Practice in Locating Fiction

OBJECTIVE

To provide practice in locating fiction books

MATERIALS

1. A chalkboard, chalk, eraser
2. Twenty 3 by 5 inch slips of paper
3. The use of a library

PREPARATIONS

1. From the library shelves, compile a list of twenty fiction titles and their authors. The authors' names should start with different letters of the alphabet to ensure that the books are spread throughout the fiction section.

2. Print, or have a student print, each of the twenty authors and titles on a separate 3 by 5 inch slip of paper like the sample below. (The format is the same as that of catalog cards.) Don't be concerned about how the titles are capitalized at this point. Librarians capitalize only first words and proper names in titles. This will be taught later on.

3. Copy the catalog card on the board.

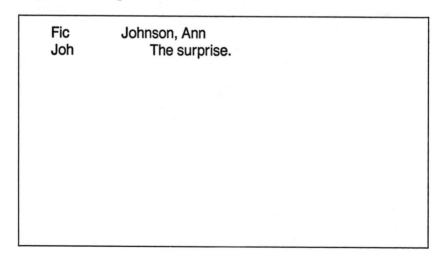

```
Fic        Johnson, Ann
Joh             The surprise.
```

4. Schedule a visit to the library. If possible, schedule a forty-five-minute period. Locating books is often challenging the first time, and you may need more than thirty minutes.

LESSON

Explain to the students that they will be going to the library today. After they arrive and sit down, assign half of the class to locate some fiction books. The other half of the class can browse and check books out. Explain that *browse* means "glance through a book or library in a leisurely way." The next time they visit the library, the groups will rotate; the group that hasn't done the assignment will do it then. Before the students go the the library, they need to do some preparing. Tell them you will be passing out some slips of paper that will tell them which books to locate, but you want to be sure they know how to read the slips.

Write a student's name on the board, e.g., Martin, John. Point to the comma.

> Do you remember what a comma in a name means?

> Yes, it means that the last name has been written first. That's important to remember.

Point to the assignment slip you copied on the board.

> This is an example of what the slips look like that I'll be giving to you.

Ask these questions:

1. What kind of book is this—easy, fiction, or a collection of stories? (fiction)
2. What is the author's name? (Ann Johnson. When reading the author's name, read the first name first.)
3. Why is there a comma after Johnson? (to warn you that the last name has been written first)
4. What is the title of the book? (*The Surprise*)
5. What does "Fic" mean? (fiction)
6. What does "Joh" stand for? (Johnson)
7. How is fiction arranged on library shelves? (by the authors' last names)
8. If you receive this slip, where in the fiction section will you look for this book? (in the "J" section)

Choose a student to carry the slips. Take the class to the library

In the Library

Seat the students.
Ask them where the fiction books are located.
Go to the first fiction section and point.

> Books are shelved by sections. You can pretend that a section is a page in a book. You read the first line from left to right. Then you go to the second line and read it from left to right. Then to the next line, and so forth.

Where do you go after you've read the last line on a page? (to the top of the next page)

Demonstrate, pointing from the last book on the bottom shelf to the first book on the top row of the next section.

Designate the beginning of fiction, and call attention to the fact that that is where books by authors whose names start with "A" will be shelved. Walk past the fiction section, calling attention to the location of the "B" authors, the "C" authors, and so forth.

Where would you look for a book by an author named Brown? (at the beginning of fiction)

Where would you look for a book by an author named Wells? (at the end of fiction)

Where would you look for a book by an author named Miller? (in the fiction section under "M"/in the middle of fiction)

I have some slips of paper on which I've written the authors and titles of the books you are to locate. Each slip names one book.

When you receive your slip, go to the shelves and find your book. Don't remove it. Touch it and hold your hand up. I will come and see if you have found the correct book. If you have, I'll give you another slip. You are to find a total of three books. If you have time after you've found your three books, you may check books out.

Announce that today the girls (or boys) will find fiction books and the boys (or girls) will browse and check books out.

Pass the slips out.

Excuse the other group.

At the end of the lesson have someone carry the slips back to the room for future use.

Next week take the class to the library and rotate the activities.

SUGGESTIONS

1. If you want to be very thorough, prepare slips for book location in the easy section. Follow the lesson plan above.

2. Thereafter you may want to mix the two sets of slips (Fic and E). Students will then have to decide whether to look in the easy or the fiction section. Try to see that each student has to look in both sections. If a student has just found an easy book, give him or her a fiction slip. The third slip could be fiction. Follow the lesson plan above. You may need to have the librarian, an aide, or a capable student help you check the students and give out slips.

Lesson 42. Nonfiction, Part I

OBJECTIVES

1. To introduce nonfiction
2. To teach how nonfiction is arranged in a library
3. To check mastery with a ditto follow-up

MATERIALS

1. Some nonfiction books (not including fairy tales, poems, plays, jokes, riddles)
2. Some fiction books
3. A chalkboard, chalk, and eraser
4. Back-to-back reproductions of Worksheets 4.9 and 4.10

PREPARATIONS

Write the following three sets on the board at a level students can reach. Leave at least 15 inches between sets. (Don't copy the answers in parentheses on the board.)

Set 1		Set 2		Set 3	
500	(300)	400	(298)	400	(220)
300	(500)	298	(400)	Z	(A)
700	(700)	786	(645)		
900	(800)	920	(786)	220	(400)
800	(900)	645	(920)	A	(Z)
				918	(796)
				N	(S)
				796	(918)
				S	(N)

LESSON

Hold up a nonfiction book.

This book is true; it's nonfiction.

"Non" means not; nonfiction means not fiction. If it's not fiction, not made up, it's true.

I'm going to hold up several books for you to see. Raise your hand when I hold up a nonfiction book.

Remember, nonfiction is true.

Hold up some fiction and nonfiction books, one at a time.

After the students have identified the nonfiction books, ask them which of the following titles are fiction and which are nonfiction.

How Bridges Are Made	(NF)
U.S. History	(NF)
The Boy Who Would Not Say His Name	(F)
Birds	(NF)
Emily's Runaway Imagination	(F)
Laura's Story	(F)
How to Play Better Soccer	(NF)
Henry and the Paper Route	(F)
All About the Moon	(NF)
Hurry Home, Candy	(F)

You can't always tell whether a book is nonfiction by its title, but many times you can.

What does nonfiction mean? (books that are true)

Although nonfiction means true, there are a few books shelved in the nonfiction section which aren't true: fairy tales, plays, poems, jokes. Nevertheless, everything shelved in the nonfiction section of a library is referred to as *nonfiction.*

There was a time when books were arranged on the shelves according to when they were acquired/obtained.

In 1876 Melvil Dewey, a twenty-five-year-old librarian, became so irritated with the illogical arrangement of books that he developed a new system.

In this new system, books are grouped by subject. Subject means what a book is about. All the books about birds are grouped together. All the books about football are grouped together, and so forth. One doesn't have to run all over a library looking for books about a certain subject, such as snakes. Once you find the snake books, you have them all. You can look through them and pick out the ones you like best.

When Mr. Dewey devised his system, he assigned numbers to every subject. Instead of writing a subject on the spine of a book, he wrote a number that represented the subject.

Under the Dewey System every subject has a specific number. Snakes are found under 598.1 (read: five ninety-eight point one). Cars are numbered 629.2 (read: six twenty-nine point two). U.S. history is in the 973s (read: nine seventy-threes).

The numbers of the Dewey System start with 000 (read: zero hundred) and go to 999 (read: nine ninety-nine).

Mr. Dewey's system is named after him: it's called the Dewey Decimal System of Classification. This system is used in nearly all school and public libraries. You'll learn more about it in the sixth grade.

You need to understand the arrangement of the Dewey Decimal System so you can locate nonfiction books.

Point to Set 1 on the board.

I've put some numbers from the Dewey System on the board, but I've mixed them up. Let's have someone come up to the board and next to the numbers, write them again, but put them in the correct order. Remember to begin with the smallest number.

Who'd like to do Set 1?

When a student has numbered the set correctly, discuss why it is correct.

Who would like to do Set 2?

Discuss how the student got the correct order.

If two numbers are the same, we decide between them by the authors' last names. The letters under the numbers in set 3 represent the authors' last names. But remember, nonfiction is shelved by number first.

Who would like to do Set 3?

Discuss the mechanics of getting the correct order.

I am going to pass out a double-sided ditto for you to do. By completing the paper, you will be able to find out how well you understand nonfiction.

Distribute the ditto.

SUGGESTION

If you have learning centers in your room or library, you may want to use this idea. Get five or six nonfiction books that *do not have decimals* in their call numbers, and put them on a learning center table. One student at a time can visit the table, put the books in the correct order, and then check his or her own work against an answer card. When finished, the student should disarrange the books so that they will be ready for the next student.

Name _____ **Date** _____

Worksheet 4.9 Arranging Nonfiction Books

Fill in the blank spaces.

1. Nonfiction is _____.

                                    true   not true

2. Nonfiction is put in order primarily (first) by _____.

                                          title   author   number

   Write these numbers in order on the spines below. The first one has been done for you.

       700   900   400   200   600   300   100

100						

Worksheet 4.10 Arranging Nonfiction Books

Write these numbers in order on the spines below. The first one has been written for you.

973	423	636	507
398	745	124	

124						

Write these numbers and authors' letters on the spines below. The first one has been done for you.

800	510	770	220
A	M	N	B
629	323	410	
C	T	L	

220						
B						

Lesson 43. Nonfiction, Part II

OBJECTIVES

1. To review nonfiction
2. To teach students how to arrange nonfiction when a decimal is involved

MATERIALS

1. A chalkboard, chalk, and eraser
2. Back-to-back reproductions of worksheets 4.11 and 4.12

LESSON

The class has learned a number of things about nonfiction. Let's see how much you remember.

Ask these questions:

1. What is nonfiction? (books that are true)
2. How is nonfiction arranged on the shelves? (by number)
3. What do the numbers represent? (subjects)
4. How would you decide which book to put first if two books both had 500 for a number? (Decide between the two by the authors' last names.)
5. Who devised the Dewey Decimal System of Classification? (Melvil Dewey/ Mr. Dewey)

You need to understand the arrangement of the Dewey Decimal System so you can find nonfiction books.

Today you'll learn how to put numbers with decimals in order.

A decimal looks like this.

Write a decimal (.) on the board.

I'm going to put three numbers on the board; one of them has a decimal. I want someone to put the numbers in order. I think you can do this without special instructions.

Write the following on the board:

598.2	(598)
598	(598.2)
599	(599)

Who would like to come up and next to the numbers, write them again, but put them in the correct order?

After someone has put the numbers on the board correctly, discuss what was done.

598 is the smallest number. 598.2 (read: five ninety-eight point two) is a tiny bit bigger than plain 598. 599 comes after both 598s.

Numbers on the right side of the decimal have a different value than numbers on the left side.

Write these numbers on the board:

629.12
629.2

The bigger number is the number on the bottom: 629.2

Cover the .12 and the .2 with your hand.

Both numbers are the same on the left side of the decimal, aren't they? Let's forget the left side and look at the right side of the decimal.

Cover the two 629s with your hand.

The first numeral has two numbers to the right of the decimal (.12). The second numeral must have two numbers to the right of the decimal also. We can't compare numerals if the number of spaces occupied after the decimal aren't equal. We will have to add a zero after the second numeral so two spaces after the decimal will be occupied.

Add a zero to 629.2 (629.20).

Which is bigger: point 12 or point 20? (point 20)

If you were looking for a book about cars that is numbered 629.2, and you gave up looking at 629.12, you wouldn't have looked far enough.

Let's try another one.

Put these numbers on the board and call on someone to come to the board and next to them, write them in order.

598.4   (598.36)
598.36   (598.4)

Let's add a zero to check.

Add a zero so that you have:

598.36
598.40

The 598s are the same.

Cover the 598s.

The number 36 comes before 40.

Write the following on the board:

973.4   (973.4)
973.76   (973.76)

Who would like to do the last one?

After the last one has been done correctly, add a zero to .4 to show that .40 is smaller than .76.

When comparing two numbers, there must always be an equal number of spaces used after the decimal.

Write on the board:

629.161
629.28

If you have these numbers, add a zero after 8 so that three spaces after the decimal are filled. With an equal number of spaces filled, you can easily see which number is bigger: 280 is bigger than 161.

When we are at the shelves comparing books that have decimals, we don't write a zero on a book, of course. We just add a zero in our minds.

State that you are going to distribute a double-sided ditto for the students to do. Pass out the reproductions of Worksheets 4.11 and 4.12.

After the assignment has been finished, put the practice items on the board, explain them, and let the students correct their own papers.

SUGGESTION

If you have learning centers in your room or library, you may want to use this idea. Get five or six nonfiction books that *have decimals* in their call numbers, and put them on a learning center table. One student at a time can visit the table, put the books in correct order, and then check his or her work against an answer card. When finished the student should disarrange the books so that they will be ready for the next student.

Note: Don't be concerned if only a few students have grasped the decimal concepts presented in this lesson. The concepts are difficult. An introduction is sufficient at this time.

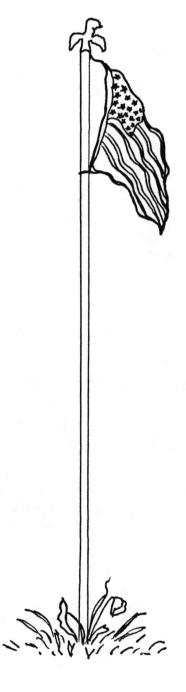

Name _____   Date _____

Worksheet 4.11 Arranging Nonfiction Books

Put these numbers in order.

Set 1   800   _____   Set 4   811.2   _____

          000   _____   811   _____

          100   _____   812   _____

          900   _____

          600   _____   Set 5   917.8   _____

                                            917.20   _____

Set 2   498   _____   917   _____

          623   _____

          918   _____   Set 6   796.23   _____

          716   _____   796   _____

          293   _____   796.3   _____

Set 3   641   _____   Set 7   636.14   _____
          C   C

          929   _____   636   _____
          B   B

          811   _____   636.3   _____
          A   A

          310   _____
          M

          525   _____
          P

Name _____   Date _____

Worksheet 4.12 Arranging Nonfiction Books

Nonfiction is arranged by number. Put these books in order by writing their call numbers in order on the lines below.

The Last Frontier	Painted Rock Creatures	Cats and Kittens	The Big Book of Horses	Bats
Adams	Lauritzen	Rockwell	Chase	Pye
979.8 Ada	745.5 Lau	636.8 Roc	636.1 Cha	599.4 Pye

1. _____

2. _____

3. _____

4. _____

5. _____

Lesson 44. Nonfiction, Part III

OBJECTIVES

1. To review nonfiction
2. To introduce the terms *call numbers* and *class numbers*
3. To introduce the reference section

MATERIALS

1. A chalkboard, chalk, and eraser
2. Reproductions of Worksheet 4.13 (quiz)

PREPARATION

Copy the following on the board.

Class numbers	636	810	918
Call numbers	636	810	918
	D	La	Gol

LESSON

Can you answer these questions?

What is nonfiction? (books that are true)

How is nonfiction arranged on the shelves? (by numbers)

Let's take a look at the numbers used in the Dewey Decimal System of Classification. You remember that a number stands for a subject.

Write 970.1 on the board and point to it.

This is the number for Indians. We call it a *class number.*

A *class number* is the number for a particular subject.

I can put the author's initial under the number and change it to a call number.

Write "S" under the number.

Let's look at some class numbers and some call numbers.

Point to the board.

Melvil Dewey grouped books into classes. These are class numbers.

Point to the class numbers on the board.

A *call number* is the class number plus one, two, or three letters from the author's name. It doesn't matter how many letters there are.

It's easy to remember which numbers are call numbers. The word *call* has the word *all* in it. The number with all the information is a call number.

I'm going to write a number on the board. Raise your hand if you can tell me if it's a class number or a call number.

Write: 423 (class number)
Call on a student to identify the number.
Continue with these numbers.

796	
C	(call number)
808	
P	(call number)
507	(class number)
999	(class number)

Most libraries have a section of reference books. Books in a reference section have special characteristics.

First, you can't check them out. They are always there in the library when you need them.

Second, reference books aren't designed to be read from cover to cover like most other books. Reference books are books that you refer to for quick information. For example, you may want to know when Abraham Lincoln was born. You probably don't want to read 300 pages to find out. You can look in a reference book and get the answer quickly.

If a book is very expensive, it is usually put in the reference section.

Reference books are nonfiction; they are true.

Some examples of reference books are dictionaries and encyclopedias.

Reference books use the same numbers that are used in nonfiction—000–999 (read: zero hundred through nine ninety-nine)—but to keep them from being shelved with the other nonfiction books an "R" is put above their numbers.

What does the "R" stand for? (reference)

Write on the board:

970.1
A

In which section would you look for this book? (nonfiction)

Add an "R" above the number you just wrote. You now have:

R
970.1
A

In which section would you look for this book? (reference)

The nonfiction section is numbered from 000–999. Reference is numbered from 000–999. Both sections are true. The two sections are separate.

I'm going to pass out a ditto. You may take out your pencil and start to work immediately unless you need to listen to me when I read the instructions.

Distribute the reproductions of Worksheet 4.13 (quiz).
Read the instructions aloud.
Correct the papers with the students, or collect, correct, and return them later.

SUGGESTION

If you have a library, point out the reference section the next time your class makes a visit.

Worksheet 4.13 Nonfiction Quiz

Match these:

1. _____ 918 S   a. a call number

2. _____ 811   b. a class number

Fill in the correct answer:

3. Books that are true are called _____.
     fiction   nonfiction

4. Books that are not true are called _____.
     fiction   nonfiction

5. Books that can't be checked out are called _____.
     fiction   reference

6. Expensive books will probably be shelved in the _____ section.
     nonfiction   reference

Are these statements about reference books *true* or *false*?

7 _____ Reference books are not true.

8. _____ They are not meant to be read all the way through.

9. _____ They are true.

10. _____ They can't be checked out.

Lesson 45. Practice in Locating Nonfiction

OBJECTIVE

To provide practice in locating nonfiction books

MATERIALS

1. A chalkboard, chalk, eraser
2. Twenty 3 by 5 inch slips of paper
3. The use of a library

PREPARATIONS

1. From the library shelves, compile a list of twenty nonfiction titles, their authors, and their call numbers. You may send two students to do this, if you prefer. The titles should be selected from throughout the nonfiction section so that when students search for books they won't all be searching in one small area.

2. Print, or have a student print, each title and its author and call number on a separate 3 by 5 inch slip of paper like the sample here. The format is the same as that of catalog cards. Don't be concerned about how the titles are capitalized at this point. (Librarians capitalize only first words and proper names in titles. This will be taught later on.)

```
598.1      Miller, John
Mil            Snakes of America.
```

3. Copy the sample slip of paper on the board.

4. Schedule a visit to the library. If possible, schedule a forty-five-minute period. Locating books is often challenging the first time, and you may need more than thirty minutes.

LESSON

Explain that the class will be going to the library today. After everyone arrives and sits down, assign half of them to locate some nonfiction books. The other half of the class can browse and check books out. The next time you visit the library, the groups will rotate. The group that didn't do the assignment will do it then. When the students get to the library, pass out some slips of paper that tell them which books to locate. First be sure that they know how to read the slips.

This is an example of what the slips look like.

Point to the slip you've copied on the board.
Ask these questions:

1. Is this book fiction or nonfiction? (nonfiction)
2. How do you know it is nonfiction? (If someone says he or she knows that it is nonfiction by the title, explain that the title is often a help, but there is something else that is more absolute. If no one knows the answer, explain that nonfiction is shelved by number. The book being considered has a number, therefore, it is nonfiction.)
3. What is the author's name? (John Miller)
4. Why is there a comma after Miller? (to warn you that the last name has been written first)
5. What is the title of the book? (*Snakes of America*)
6. What do the letters "Mil" stand for? (the first three letters of the author's last name)
7. What does the number 598.1 stand for? (the subject, which is snakes, and where the book is shelved)
8. How is nonfiction arranged on library shelves? (by number)
9. Where in the library would you look for this book? (in the nonfiction section)

Choose a student to carry the slips. Take the class to the library.

In the Library

Seat the students.
Ask the students where the fiction books are located.
Designate the beginning of nonfiction. Walk from the beginning to the end. As you walk, point out the different sections.

Here are the 000s (read: zero hundreds), the 100s, the 200s, the 300s, the 400s, the 500s, the 600s, the 700s, the 800s, and the 900s.

Ask where a student should start looking for the snake book. (in the 500s *or* in the middle of the nonfiction section)

Tell the students that you will pass some slips of paper to half of them. Each slip gives the title, author, and call number of a book that is to be located.

> When you receive a slip of paper, go to the shelves and locate your book. Don't remove it from the shelf. Touch it and hold your hand up. I'll come and see if you have found the correct book. If you have, I'll give you another slip. You are to find a total of three books. If you have time after you've found your three books, you may check a book out.

Announce that today the boys (or girls) will find nonfiction books as you've described and the girls (or boys) will browse and check books out. Distribute the slips. Excuse the group that has been assigned to locate books. When that group has gone to the shelves, excuse the group that is going to browse and check books out.

Save the slips for future use.

FOLLOW-UP

Next week review the concepts taught in this lesson before going to the library and rotating the groups.

Hereafter you may want to mix the nonfiction and fiction slips (or the nonfiction, fiction, and easy slips) and take the students to the library for more book location lessons similar to the one above. You will probably need help in checking the students. Perhaps you can get the librarian, an aide, or a capable student to help.

Lesson 46. The Card Catalog, Part I

OBJECTIVES

1. To introduce the card catalog
2. To present the rules for finding author, subject, and title cards in the card catalog
3. To provide practice in selecting appropriate card catalog drawers

MATERIALS

1. A chalkboard, chalk, and eraser
2. Three 3 by 5 inch catalog cards, file cards, or slips of paper
3. A hardback and paperback book
4. Reproductions of Worksheet 4.14

PREPARATION

Copy this card catalog on the board. Alternative: Pass out copies of Worksheet 4.14 and let students refer to the card catalog at the top during your presentation. (The students' pencils should be inside their desks during the lesson.)

A	D	H	M	S
B	E-F	I-K	N-P	T-U
C	G	L	Q-R	V-Z

LESSON

Point to the card catalog on the board, or if you're using the picture of the card catalog on Worksheet 4.14, refer to it.

> Every library has an index to its book collection. Usually the index is in the form of a card catalog. An index, such as the card catalog, will tell you where to find the books you want.

> The card catalog is made up of a number of drawers. Each drawer is full of cards.

Hold up three 3 by 5 inch catalog cards, file cards, or slips of paper.

> The cards are this size.

> Let's pretend that the librarian has just received a book titled *Black Stallion.* He or she knows that someone will come to the library looking for that book by title, so the librarian files a card in the card catalog under *Black Stallion.*

> The next person who comes to the library may want a fiction book about horses. Maybe the person doesn't know the title of a particular book but only knows the subject. Subject means what the book is about. The librarian files a card for that person under the subject: HORSES—STORIES.

> Another person may have read a number of books by Walter Farley and may think, "I like Walter Farley's books. I wonder if he has written any books that I haven't read yet?" The librarian knows that someone may look under the author's name, so he or she files a card under Walter Farley.

The librarian files a card under the title, the author, and the subject for every hardback book in the library. So if you know the title, the author, or the subject of a book, you can find it by using the card catalog.

Hold up a hardback book.

A hardback book looks like this.

Hold up a paperback book.

A paperback book has soft paper covers.

All of the books in the library are indexed in the card catalog except paperbacks.

Can you guess how the cards in the card catalog are arranged? (in alphabetical order)

The labels on each drawer tell you which cards are filed inside.

Look at the card catalog on the board (or on your ditto).

Ask these questions:

1. In which drawer of the card catalog would you look for a book about dinosaurs? (D)
2. Mice? (M)
3. Football? (E–F)
4. Snakes (S)
5. Baseball? (B)

Explain that author cards are filed under the author's last name.
Ask these questions.

1. In which drawer of the card catalog would you look for a book by Marcia Brown? (B)
2. Mildred Taylor (T–U)
3. Elizabeth Speare (S)
4. Carolyn Haywood (H)
5. Robert Lawson (L)

Explain that title cards are filed under the first word of a book's title.
The words *a, an,* and *the* are not used as first words of a title; they are disregarded.
To make a visual impression, write these words on the board: a, an, the.
Ask these questions.
In which drawer would you look for each of these titles?

1. *Green Eggs and Ham* (G)
2. *Raggedy Ann and Andy* (Q–R)
3. *The Wizard of Oz* (V–Z)
4. *Aventures of Pinocchio* (A)
5. *A Book of Dragons* (B)
6. *Five Chinese Brothers* (E–F)
7. *An Eagle's Journey* (E–F)

> If you are going to look up an author in the card catalog, would you look under his or her first or last name? (last name)

Explain that people are always listed by last names in roll books, telephone books, encyclopedias, and so forth.

> If you're going to look up a title in a card catalog, which word would you look under? (the first, disregarding the words *a, an, the*)

To make this easy to remember, explain that some titles have only one word.

> The rule has to be easy so millions of people can remember it.

> The rule has to be the same for all titles. We can't say look under the sixth word. Some titles don't have six words.

> How do you find a title in the card catalog? (Look under the first word of the title, disregarding the words *a, an, the.*)

Tell the students that you are going to have them do a ditto so they can practice using what they have just learned.

If you haven't distributed Worksheet 4.14, do so now.

> Notice that titles of books are underlined.

> Start to work.

Correct the papers with the students, explaining each item as you go.

Note: Item 7 on the worsheet, *George Washington*, may cause difficulty. Explain that *George Washington* is underlined, so it's a title. Titles are filed under their first words.

Worksheet 4.14 The Card Catalog

A	D	H	M	S
B	E-F	I-K	N-P	T-U
C	G	L	Q-R	V-Z

In which drawer will you find a card for each of these?

1. Dogs _____

2. The Girl Who Loved Wild Horses _____

3. Don Freeman _____

4. Birds _____

5. Little Red Hen _____

6. Shirley Jackson _____

7. George Washington _____

8. A Chair for My Mother _____

9. Jokes _____

10. An Evergreen Tree for Christmas _____

Lesson 47. The Card Catalog, Part II

OBJECTIVES

1. To review the use of the card catalog
2. To review how author, title, and subject catalog cards are filed
3. To provide practice in selecting appropriate catalog card drawers

MATERIALS

1. A chalkboard, chalk, and eraser
2. Reproductions of Worksheet 4.15

PREPARATION

Copy this card catalog on the board. Alternative: Pass out copies of Worksheet 4.15 and let students refer to the card catalog at the top during your presentation. (The students' pencils should be inside their desks during the lesson.)

A-B	I-K	Q-S
C-E	L-M	T-V
F-H	N-P	W-Z

LESSON

Who remembers how the card catalog helps us? (It tells us where to find books.)

What do you need to know about a book to be able to find it in the card catalog? (author, title, or subject)

Which books are not indexed in the card catalog? (paperbacks)

If you're going to use the ditto picture of the card catalog instead of drawing on the board, pass out copies of Worksheet 4.15 now.

Notice that the card catalog drawn on the board (on your ditto) is a little different from the one we looked at last time. In this catalog each drawer contains cards for two or more letters. The cards starting with the letters "A" and "B" are in the first drawer. Cards starting with letters "C"–"E," meaning letters "C," "D," and "E," are in the second drawer, and so forth.

Ask these questions:

1. In which drawer of the card catalog would you look for a book about dogs? (the one labeled C–E)
2. Rabbits (Q–S)
3. Ocean (N–P)
4. Goats (F–H)
5. United States (T–V)
6. How are author cards filed? (by the authors' last names)
7. In which drawer would you look for Judy Blume? (A–B)
8. Paul Galdone (F–H)
9. Lillian Hoban (F–H)
10. Arnold Lobel (L–M)
11. Brian Wildsmith (W–Z)
12. How are title cards filed? (under the first word of the title)
13. Which three words are disregarded when they are the first words in a title? (a, an, the)
14. In which drawer would you look for *Mr. Popper's Penguins* (L–M)
15. *Sounder* (Q–S)
16. *Dear Mr. Henshaw* (C–E)
17. *A Wrinkle in Time* (W–Z)
18. *The Twenty-One Balloons* (T–V)
19. *An Evening in Paris* (C–E)
20. *Ramona the Pest* (Q–S)

Are author cards filed under the author's first or last name? (last)

How are title cards filed? (under the first word of the title)

Which three words are disregarded as first words in a title? (a, an, the)

Take out your pencils and do the ditto, which I'm going to pass out (I've passed out).

Worksheet 4.15 The Card Catalog

A-B	I-K	Q-S
C-E	L-M	T-V
F-H	N-P	W-Z

In which drawer will you find a card for each of these?

1. Strawberry Girl _____

2. George Selden _____

3. The Sneetches and Other Stories _____

4. Young Fu of the Upper Yangtze _____

5. Beverly Cleary _____

6. A Very Merry Cricket _____

7. Up a Road Slowly _____

8. An Ocean Voyage _____

9. Elizabeth Yates _____

10. King of the Wind _____

Lesson 48. The Card Catalog, Part III

OBJECTIVES

1. To review the use of the card catalog
2. To introduce the card catalog's guide cards
3. To give practice using guide cards

MATERIALS

1. A chalkboard, chalk, and eraser
2. Back-to-back reproductions of Worksheets 4.16 and 4.17

PREPARATION

Copy this catalog drawer on the board.

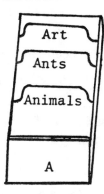

LESSON

You've been learning about the card catalog.

Who remembers how the card catalog helps us? (It tells us where to find the books we want.)

How many catalog cards do most books have? (three)

What might you know about a book that would enable you to find it through the card catalog? (author, title, or subject)

If you get one answer, keep eliciting answers until you get all three—author, subject, title. If the students can give only two answers, you may have to tell them the third.

You've learned how to use the labels on the card catalog drawers. Today you're going to learn how to use the guide cards, which are inside the drawers.

I'm going to pass out a ditto, which has a picture of a drawer and some guide cards. Don't take your pencils out of your desks.

Distribute reproductions of Worksheets 4.16 and 4.17.

Look at the picture on Worksheet 4.16.

See the cards that are standing higher than the others? Those are guide cards.

Who would like to read the guide cards aloud?

When you are looking for a specific card in a drawer, it is hard to find it among hundreds of cards. Guide cards help you find the card you want. They let you know where you are alphabetically.

If you want to find a book about ants, you won't have to look through the hundreds of cards in the "A" drawer. You will look at the six guide cards. You will ask yourself, "Between which of those six cards will I find the subject *ants?*"

Ants is listed on your worksheet. Look at item 1.

Who can tell me between which guide cards *ants* will be found? (animals and art)

Yes, *ants* comes alphabetically after *animals* but before *art*. Let's look closely at these three words.

Point to the board.

I've drawn a picture of a catalog drawer, two guide cards, and the card we want: ants. You can see that *ants* comes between *animals* and *art*.

Let's look a little closer and prove that *ants* comes between *animals* and *art*. All three words start with "a." Let's cross "a" off.

Draw a line through the first letter ("a") in each word, as follows:

art
ants
animals

Now look at the second letter of each word. The "n"s come before "r." Let's erase the word *art*. We know it's last.

Which of the words with "n" comes first? (animals)

Let's look at the board at the third letters. We have a "t" and an "i."

Which comes first? ("i")

Animals comes before *ants* and *art* comes after *ants*.

See how much easier it is to look between the two guide cards than it is to look through the whole drawer?

Look at the guide cards again. The first card is just plain "A." But notice that all the other cards have important subjects on them: Africa, America, Animals, Art, Automobiles. If you're looking for an important subject, often it'll be listed right on a guide card. Then you can find that subject very fast, can't you?

Guide cards help us in two ways: They help us alphabetically so we can locate any card, and they give us especially quick help in locating important subjects.

Look at item 2 on your worksheet: America.

Between which guide cards would you find America? (America and Animals)

In all of the following examples, if you feel there is a need, write the card being sought on the board and put the two guide cards the student has chosen above and below it. Then show how to determine if the student has alphabetized correctly by drawing lines through the letters as was done with the card for ants. (Do all of Worksheet 4.16 orally.)

You can see how important it is to know the alphabet well, can't you? If you don't know the alphabet, you can't find cards in the card catalog or books in the library. If you don't know the alphabet, you won't even be able to use a telephone book. You won't be able to look up your friend's phone number.

Let's review the rules for finding author, subject, and title cards in the card catalog.

When you are looking for a subject, you look directly under the subject. For example, if you want a book about butterflies, you look under *butterflies*.

If you are looking for an author, should you look under his or her first or last name? (last)

How are title cards filed? (under the first word of the title)

Which three words do we disregard if they are the first words of a title? (a, an, the)

We've practiced using guide cards together. Now let's see whether you can use guide cards by yourself.

Assign Worksheet 4.17. Alternatives: Assign Worksheets 4.16 and 4.17, or assign Worksheet 4.16 one day and Worksheet 4.17 on another day.

Worksheet 4.16 Guide Cards

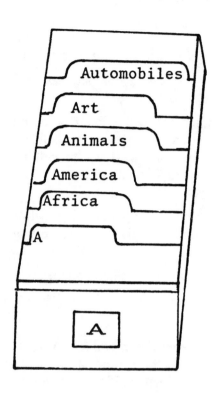

Between which guide cards would you find these?

1. Ants   _____   _____

2. America   _____   _____

3. Animal Babies   _____   _____

4. Adrienne Adams   _____   _____

5. Across Five Aprils   _____   _____

6. Are You My Mother?   _____   _____

7. Robert Arthur   _____   _____

8. Astronauts   _____   _____

9. Acting   _____   _____

10. Alice in Wonderland   _____   _____

Name _____   Date _____

Worksheet 4.17 Guide Cards

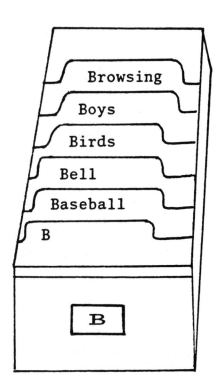

Between which guide cards would you find these?

1. Backpacking   _____   _____

2. Brazil   _____   _____

3. Jeanne Bendick   _____   _____

4. Bambi   _____   _____

5. Books   _____   _____

6. Bees   _____   _____

7. Bears   _____   _____

8. Margaret Wise Brown   _____   _____

9. Robert Bright   _____   _____

10. Bird Nests   _____   _____

Lesson 49. The Card Catalog, Part IV

OBJECTIVES

1. To review the use of the card catalog
2. To review how author, title, and subject cards are filed
3. To give the students practice in using guide cards

MATERIALS

1. A chalkboard, chalk, and eraser
2. Back-to-back reproductions of Worksheets 4.18 and 4.19

PREPARATION

Copy onto the board the card catalog drawer and guide cards on Worksheet 4.18. Alternative: Pass out copies of the worksheet and let students refer to the guide cards at the top during your presentation. (The students' pencils should be inside their desks during the lesson.)

LESSON

Let's review what you've learned about the card catalog.

Ask these questions:

1. How does the card catalog help us? (It helps us locate books.)
2. What do you need to know about a book to be able to find it through the card catalog? (the author, title, or subject)
3. How do you find books about a certain subject? (Look under the subject.)
4. If you're looking for an author in the card catalog, should you look under the author's first or last name? (last)
5. If you're looking for a title, what do you look under in the card catalog? (the first word of the title)
6. Which three words are disregarded if they're first words in titles? (a, an, the)
7. How do guide cards help us? (They help us alphabetically in finding a card. They also help us find important subjects quickly.)

Let's look at the guide cards on the board (on your ditto).

Between which cards would you find *rocks?* (Rivers and Rome)

If you need to, explain the alphabetizing in minute detail. See Lesson 48 for the method.

> Between which cards would you find *Rabbit Hill?* (R and Railroads)
>
> Louise Rich? (Reptiles and Rivers)
>
> Riddles? (Reptiles and Rivers)
>
> Jack Ryan? (after Rome)
>
> I'd like for you to do some practice items on your own now.
>
> When you look at each item, ask yourself if you are looking for a subject. If you are, look directly under the subject.
>
> If you are looking for an author, look under the author's last name.
>
> If you are looking for a title, look under the first word, except you must disregard the words *a, an,* and *the* when they are first words.
>
> Watch your alphabetizing very carefully.

If you haven't distributed the back-to-back reproduction of the worksheets, do so now.

SUGGESTION

Work on alphabetizing daily. Have students alphabetize their spelling words. Buy a ditto book of alphabetizing lessons. Drill. Drill. Drill.

Worksheet 4.18 Guide Cards

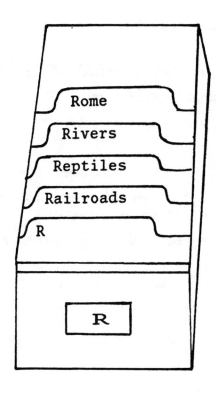

Between which guide cards would you find these?

1. <u>Raggedy Ann and Andy</u> —————————— ——————————

2. Rocks —————————— ——————————

3. Ruth Robbins —————————— ——————————

4. <u>Rip Van Winkle</u> —————————— ——————————

5. Roosters—Stories —————————— ——————————

6. <u>Return of the Jedi</u> —————————— ——————————

7. Reindeer —————————— ——————————

8. <u>Ramona Forever</u> —————————— ——————————

9. Bill Richardson —————————— ——————————

10. Jane Radford —————————— ——————————

Name _____   Date _____

Worksheet 4.19 Guide Cards

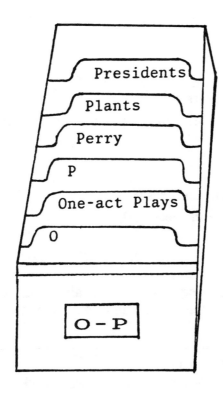

Between which guide cards would you find these?

1. Octopus _____   _____

2. The Old Woman and Her Pig _____   _____

3. Peggy Parish _____   _____

4. Fritz Peters _____   _____

5. Ox-Cart Man _____   _____

6. Poetry _____   _____

7. Police _____   _____

8. Puppets and puppet plays _____   _____

9. Paper Crafts _____   _____

10. Put Me in the Zoo _____   _____

Lesson 50. Card Catalog Review and Practice, Part I

OBJECTIVES

1. To review the card catalog
2. To provide practice in reading and understanding catalog cards

MATERIALS

1. A chalkboard, chalk, and eraser
2. Reproductions of Worksheet 4.20

PREPARATION

Copy the following catalog card on the chalkboard. Leave room between the top of the card and the first line for one additional line of writing.

```
Fic        Brown, Ed
Bro            A dog for Johnny; illustrated by
           Tim Wells. Wayside Press 1986
               160p.    illus.
```

LESSON

Let's review what you've learned about the card catalog.

Ask these questions:

1. What is the purpose of a card catalog? (to tell you where to find the book you want)
2. How is it arranged? (in alphabetical order)
3. What three things can you know about a book that will enable you to locate it through the card catalog? (author, subject, title)
4. If you want to look up an author in the card catalog, should you look under his or her first or last name? (last)
5. If you want to look up a title in the card catalog, which word of the title should you look under? (first)
6. Which three words do we disregard as first words of a title? (a, an, the)

If you learn how to read and understand catalog cards, you'll be able to find books for yourself.

Point to the catalog card on the board.

Here is what a catalog card looks like. Of course, it isn't this big.

If you have put a ragged bottom edge on your catalog card, explain that the ragged edge means that you've shortened the card.

Let's see if you understand this catalog card.

Ask these questions:

1. What is the title of the book? (*A Dog for Johnny*)

Librarians don't capitalize titles like most people do; librarians capitalize only proper nouns and first words in titles.

Continue your questions. Point to the parts being considered.

2. Who do you think Ed Brown is? (the author)
3. What does "Fic" mean? (fiction)
4. What does "Bro" stand for? (Brown)
5. Who illustrated the book? (Tim Wells)
6. What does "illustrated" mean? (Pictures were drawn.)
7. Who is the publisher? (Wayside Press)
8. What is the copyright date? (1986)
9. How many pages are in the book? (160)
10. What does "p" after the number 160 mean? (pages)
11. What does "illus.," the last word on the card, mean? (There are illustrations in the book.)
12. Where in the library would you look for this book? (in the fiction section under Brown)

The information in the left corner of the card tells you where to find the book.

Point.

You can tell whether a card is an author, subject, or title card by the first line. If the author's name is on the first line, you have an author card. If the title is on the first line, you have a title card. If the subject is on the first line, you have a subject card. Because it might be difficult to tell the difference between a title and a subject card, every letter of the subject is capitalized. Complete capitalization of the first line means you are not looking at a title but at a subject.

13. What kind of card is on the board? (author)
14. How do you know? (The author's name is on the top line.)

Write this on the board above Brown, Ed: A dog for Johnny. (Note: The title appears twice on the card now.)

15. What kind of card is this now? (title card)

Erase the line you just wrote and put the following in its place: DOGS—STORIES. Be sure to print this line in full capitals.

16. What kind of card is this now? (subject)
17. How do you know? (The first line is capitalized.)

> What can you know about a book that will enable you to locate it by using the card catalog? (author, title, or subject)
>
> I'm going to distribute a ditto that shows examples of the three catalog cards that usually come with a book.

Distribute reproductions of Worksheet 4.20.

> On this ditto there are examples of three catalog cards. There is an author card, a title card, and a subject card. The first line tells you what kind of card you are looking at. If the author is on the first line, you are looking at an author card. If the title is on the first line, you are looking at a title card. If the subject is on the first line, you are looking at a subject card.
>
> The librarian capitalizes every letter of the subject. This tells you this is not the title; it's the subject.

Ask these questions about the ditto.

1. Which card on the worksheet is a title card? (the second)
2. Which card is an author card? (the first)
3. Which card is a subject card? (the third)
4. How do you know the third card is the subject card? (Every letter on the first line is capitalized.)
5. What is the title of the book? (*The First Book of Horses*)
6. Who is the author? (Janet White)
7. What is the call number? (636.1 Whi)
8. Is the book fiction or nonfiction? (nonfiction)

9. How do you know? (It has a number.)
10. What does "Whi" stand for? (White)
11. How many pages are in the book? (232)
12. Who illustrated the book? (Roy Turner)
13. What is the copyright date? (1986)
14. Who is the publisher? (Silver Press)
15. Are there any pictures? (yes)
16. How do you know? (The card says illustrated by Roy Turner, and it says illustrations.)

Collect the dittos.

Worksheet 4.20 The Card Catalog

636.1   White, Janet
Whi   The first book of horses;
illus. by Roy Turner. Silver
Press 1986
    232p.   illus.

The first book of horses

636.1   White, Janet
Whi   The first book of horses;
illus. by Roy Turner. Silver
Press 1986
    232p.   illus.

HORSES

636.1   White, Janet
Whi   The first book of horses;
illus. by Roy Turner. Silver
Press 1986
    232p.   illus.

Lesson 51. Card Catalog Review and Practice, Part II

OBJECTIVES

1. To review the card catalog
2. To provide practice in reading and understanding catalog cards

MATERIALS

1. A chalkboard, chalk, and eraser
2. Back-to-back reproductions of Worksheets 4.21 and 4.22

PREPARATION

Put the following catalog card on the chalkboard. Leave room between the author's name (Woods, Ted) and the top of the card for one additional line of writing.

```
  E        Woods, Ted
  Woo            Ten miles from home; illus. by
           Dan Shaw.    J. P. Bright   1982
               32p.    illus.
```

LESSON

We're going to continue our study of catalog cards.

Look at the catalog card on the board.

Ask these questions.

1. Who is the illustrator of this book? (Dan Shaw)
2. How many pages are there? (32 pages)
3. What is the title? (*Ten Miles from Home*)
4. Who is the author? (Ted Woods)
5. Who is the publisher? (J. P. Bright)

6. Is the book nonfiction? (no)

7. Is it from the easy, fiction, or story collection section of the library? (easy)

8. How do we know? (by the "E")

9. What does "Woo" stand for? (Woods)

10. What does "illus." on the last line mean? (illustrations—there are illustrations)

11. What is the copyright date? (1982)

12. Is this an author, title, or subject card? (author card—the author's name is on the first line)

Write the title on the board, inside the card, but above the author's name, as shown:

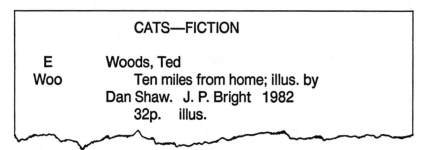

```
                    Ten miles from home

        E         Woods, Ted
        Woo           Ten miles from home; illus. by
                  Dan Shaw.    J. P. Bright    1982
                      32p.    illus.
```

What kind of card is this now? (title)

Erase the title you just wrote and write in the same place: CATS—FICTION, as shown below. (Be sure that you write this in full capitals.)

```
                    CATS—FICTION

        E         Woods, Ted
        Woo           Ten miles from home; illus. by
                  Dan Shaw.   J. P. Bright   1982
                      32p.    illus.
```

What kind of card is this now? (subject card)

How do you know? (All the letters on the first line are capitalized.)

I'm going to pass out a double-sided ditto.

Distribute back-to-back reproductions of Worksheets 4.21 and 4.22.

Look at Worksheet 4.21. The cards pictured are a set: they are for the same book.

Ask these questions.

1. What is the title of the book? (*Charlotte's Web*)

2. Who is the author? (E. B. White)

3. Who is the illustrator? (Garth Williams)

4. How many pages are in the book? (184 pages)

5. Who published the book? (Harper and Row)

6. What is the copyright date? (1952)

7. What does "Whi" stand for? (White)

8. Are there illustrations? (yes)

9. How do you know? (The card says pictures by Garth Williams, and on the last line it says illustrations.)

10. What kind of card is the first one? (author)

Inform the students that the information at the bottom of the card is for the librarian's use. They do not need to read that part of the card.

11. Which card is a subject card? (the last card)

12. How do you know? (Every letter on the first line is capitalized.)

13. Which card is a title card? (the second card)

14. How can you tell whether a card is an author, subject, or title card? (by what's on the first line)

15. Where would you find this book in the library? (in the fiction section under "W")

16. How do you know? (The left-hand corner of the card says "Whi," which refers to the author's last name, White. Fiction is shelved by author.)

If a book has several subjects, it may have not only an author, title, and subject card. It may have several subject cards. Some books have illustrator cards. Some have series cards.

Turn your papers over to Worksheet 4.22. Answer the questions.

Correct the papers with the students, or collect, correct, and return them later.

Worksheet 4.21 The Card Catalog

Whi   White, E. B.
            Charlotte's web; pictures by
      Garth Williams.   Harper & Row
      1952
            184p.   illus.

        1 Pigs—Stories 2   Spiders—
      Stories   I   Illus   II   T

              Charlotte's web

Whi   White, E. B.
            Charlotte's web; pictures by
      Garth Williams.   Harper & Row
      1952
            184p.   illus.

        1 Pigs—Stories 2   Spiders—
      Stories   I   Illus   II   T

              PIGS—STORIES

Whi   White, E. B.
            Charlotte's web; pictures by
      Garth Williams.   Harper & Row
      1952
            184p.   illus.

        1 Pigs—Stories 2   Spiders—
      Stories   I   Illus   II   T

Worksheet 4.22   The Card Catalog

```
Spe          Speare, Elizabeth George
                The sign of the beaver.
             Houghton Mifflin   1983
                135p.
```

1. What is the title of the book? _____

2. Who is the author? _____

3. What is the call number? _____

4. Who is the publisher? _____

5. How many pages are in the book? _____

6. What is the copyright date? _____

7. What does "Spe" mean? _____

8. Is the book fiction or nonfiction? _____

9. How do you know? _____

    _____

10. Are there any illustrations? _____

Lesson 52. Card Catalog Review and Practice, Part III

OBJECTIVES

1. To review catalog cards
2. To provide practice in reading and understanding catalog cards

MATERIALS

1. A chalkboard, chalk, and eraser
2. Back-to-back reproductions of Worksheets 4.23 and 4.24

PREPARATION

Copy the following catalog card on the chalkboard. Leave room between the top of the card and the first line for one additional line of writing.

```
Fic        Baxter, Paul
Bax             A home in the mountains;
           illus. by Pat Jackson. Three
           Rivers Press    1986
                unp.    illus.
```

LESSON

Today we're going to review catalog cards.

Look at the catalog card on the board.

Ask these questions.

1. What's the title of the book? (*A Home in the Mountains*)
2. Who is the publisher? (Three Rivers Press)
3. Who is the illustrator? (Pat Jackson)
4. What does "illus." on the last line mean? (There are illustrations, which means there are pictures.)
5. Who is the author? (Paul Baxter)
6. What is the call number? (Fic Bax)

7. Is the book fiction or nonfiction? (fiction)

8. How do you know? ("Fic" in the left corner means fiction. Nonfiction books have numbers.)

9. What does "Bax" stand for? (Baxter)

10. What kind of card is this? (author)

> Some books have unnumbered pages. In such cases, the person who is making the catalog cards doesn't take time to count all of the pages, he or she just writes unpaged (unp.) on the catalog cards.
>
> Notice the letters "unp.," which stand for unpaged.

Write the subject on the board inside the card above the author's name. Be sure you write this in full capitals. Example:

```
                          MOUNTAIN LIFE—FICTION

        Fic        Baxter, Paul
        Bax                A home in the mountains;
                   illus. by Pat Jackson.    Three Rivers
                   Press    1986
                         unp.    illus.
```

What kind of card is this now? (subject)

How do you know? (because the top line is in capitals)

Erase the subject you just wrote, and write the title in its place. Example:

```
                          A home in the mountains

        Fic        Baxter, Paul
        Bax                A home in the mountains;
                   illus. by Pat Jackson.    Three Rivers
                   Press    1986
                         unp.    illus.
```

What kind of card is this now? (title)

How do you know? (The title is on the first line.)

I'm going to distribute a double-sided ditto.

Pass out the reproductions of Worksheets 4.23 and 4.24.

Look at Worksheet 4.23.

Notice that the cards are for three different books.

Ask these questions.

1. Which card is a title card? (the first one)
2. How do you know? (The title is on the first line.)
3. Which card is an author card? (the third one)
4. How do you know? (The author's name is on the top line.)
5. Which card is a subject card? (the second one)
6. How do you know it's a subject card? (The top line is in capitals.)

Look again at the first card.

Ask these questions.

1. What is the title of the book? (*Dick Whittington and His Cat*)
2. Who is the author? (Marcia Brown, technically speaking, since Marcia Brown is retelling the story.)
3. Who is the illustrator? (Marcia Brown)
4. How many pages are in the book? (The book is unpaged.)
5. What does "illus." on the last line mean? (There are pictures—illustrations—in the book.)
6. Who is the publisher? (Charles Scribner's Sons)
7. What is the copyright date? (1950)
8. What is the call number? (398 Bro)
9. Is the book fiction or nonfiction? (nonfiction)
10. How do you know? (It has a number in the left corner.)
11. What does "Bro" under 398 mean? (Brown)
12. Were the illustrations painted? (no)

The card tells us that Marcia Brown cut the pictures in linoleum.

Explain what linoleum is.

Look at the second card.

Ask these questions.

1. Who is the author of the book? (Katherine Evans, technically speaking, since Katherine Evans is retelling a folk tale.)
2. Who published the book? (Whitman)
3. What is the copyright date? (1964)
4. What's the call number? (398.2 Eva)
5. What does "Eva" refer to? (Evans)
6. Who is the illustrator? (Katherine Evans)
7. What is the title? (*One Good Deed Deserves Another*)
8. How many pages are in the book? (The book is unpaged.)
9. What does "illus." on the last line mean? (There are pictures—illustrations—in the book.)
10. Is the book fiction or nonfiction? (nonfiction)
11. How do you know? (It has a number in the left corner.)
12. What is the subject of this book? (Mexican folklore)

Now look at the third card.

Ask these questions.

1. What is the title of the book? (*Sounder*)
2. What is the call number? (Fic Arm)
3. Who is the author? (William Howard Armstrong)
4. Who is the publisher? (Harper)
5. What is the copyright date? (1969)
6. Who is the illustrator? (James Barkley)
7. How many pages are in the book? (116 pages)
8. What does "illus." on the last line mean? (There are illustrations—pictures—in the book.)
9. What does "Arm" refer to? (Armstrong)
10. What does "Fic" stand for? (fiction)

Turn your papers over to the other side, and take your pencils out and start working on Worksheet 4.24.

Correct the papers with the students, or collect, correct, and return them later.

Worksheet 4.23 The Card Catalog

Dick Whittington and his cat

398 Brown, Marcia
Bro   Dick Whittington and his cat.
Told and cut in linoleum by Marcia
Brown.   Charles Scribner's Sons
1950
        unp. illus.

FOLKLORE—MEXICO

398.2 Evans, Katherine
Eva   One good deed deserves another;
retold and illus. by Katherine
Evans.   Whitman 1964
        unp.   illus.

Fic   Armstrong, William Howard
Arm   Sounder; illus. by James Barkley.
Harper   1969
        116p.   illus.

Name _____   Date _____

Worksheet 4.24 The Card Catalog

```
Spe         Sperry, Armstrong
                Call it courage.     Illus. by
            the author.   Macmillan     1940
                95p.    illus.
```

1. What is the copyright date? _____

2. Who is the publisher? _____

3. What is the title? _____

_____

4. What is the call number? _____

5. What does "illus." on the last line mean? _____

_____

6. Who is the author? _____

7. How many pages are in the book? _____

8. Is the book fiction or nonfiction? _____

9. What does "Spe" stand for? _____

_____

10. Who is the illustrator? _____

Lesson 53. Card Catalog Practice in the Library

OBJECTIVE

To give practice using the card catalog

MATERIALS

1. A card catalog
2. A chalkboard, chalk, and eraser
3. Twenty 3 by 5 inch slips of paper
4. Pencils
5. Reproductions of Worksheet 4.25, cut in half.

PREPARATIONS

1. Go to your school library and find out how many drawers the card catalog
   has. The number will determine how many of your students can use the
   card catalog at a time. If there are fifteen drawers and you have thirty
   students, half of your students can use the card catalog during the first visit
   and the other half can use it on your next visit. If there are ten drawers,
   plan to have a class of thirty rotate during three visits. Don't have more
   than half of your students use the card catalog at a time.

2. List one subject from each drawer of the card catalog on a separate 3 by 5
   inch slip of paper.

   The card catalog at my school has 20 drawers. The subjects below are the
   ones I use. You may want to see if they will help you in making your list.
   Choose only one subject per drawer. Check to see that there is a card for the
   subject.

ALASKA	FOXES	LINCOLN	SEALS
BASKETBALL	GREECE	MEXICO	SUBMARINES
CATS	HURRICANES	NETHERLANDS	TREES
DUCKS	INDIA	PERU	VOLCANOES
EGYPT	KITES	REINDEER	ZOO

3. Schedule the two or three visits you will need to complete the lesson. A
   week between visits works well.

4. Copy the ditto reproduction on the board. (In other words, copy one-half of
   Worksheet 4.25 on the board.)

5. If the librarian or library clerk can help you during your lesson, arrange for this now. It can be difficult for the teacher to assist half a class without help.

6. Copy the card catalog drawer and guide cards below on the board.

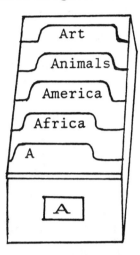

7. Copy the following catalog card on the board.

> 551.21   Carson, James
> Car   Volcanoes.   Bookwright Press
>   1983
>   48p.   illus.

LESSON

In the Classroom

Tell the students that they will be going to the library today. Explain that one-half (one-third) of them will do an assignment in which they will use the card catalog, and the other one-half (two-thirds) of the class will browse and look for books to check out. Say that those students who don't get to do the assignment today will get to do it in the future.

> Your assignment is to locate a book on the subject listed on the slip of paper you'll receive. You are to begin your search by looking in the card catalog.

Tell the class how many drawers are in the card catalog.
Explain that you have chosen one subject from each drawer.
Hold up a 3 by 5 inch slip of paper.

> The paper I'm holding says "Alaska."
>
> In which drawer will Alaska be found? (A)
>
> Usually one doesn't take a catalog drawer away from the area where the catalog is located. However, I have reserved the library just for our class, and since we are doing a practice exercise, you have permission to take the drawers to the tables that I will designate.
>
> Those who will be doing the assignment are to sit together so I can help you.
>
> I've put a copy of the assignment paper on the board.

Point to the appropriate lines as you speak.

> Write your name at the top of the assignment paper.
>
> Then write the subject that appears on your slip of paper.
>
> Go to the card catalog and get the appropriate drawer. Look at the guide cards and then the catalog cards until you find your subject. Choose one card and stay with that card. You can't take information off of two different cards.
>
> Copy the author, title, and call number from the card.
>
> Then put the drawer back.
>
> Give your 3 by 5 inch slip to me.
>
> Go to the shelves and find the book you have recorded on your assignment paper. Touch the book and raise your hand. Don't remove the book. You will be checked by me (the librarian, the aide, a designated student). Afterward you may look for a book to check out.
>
> You may keep your assignment paper after I've seen it.
>
> Now before we start, we need to review two things so you will be able to do this assignment.
>
> First, let's review how to use guide cards. Remember, you aren't going to look through 1,000 cards to find your subject. You will examine the five or six guide cards in the appropriate drawer and decide between which ones you should look.
>
> I've put some sample guide cards on the board.
>
> Between which cards would you look for Alaska? (between Africa and America)

Would it be easier to look between the two guide cards (point) or would it be easier to look through all the cards in the drawer? (between the two guide cards)

Remember to use the guide cards.

Second, we need to review a catalog card. Look at the one I've put on the board.

You will need to find the author, title, and call number.

Who is the author of this book? (James Carson)

What is the title? (*Volcanoes*)

What is the call number? (551.21 Car)

You will find that the actual catalog card will be more difficult to read than the card I have put on the board.

I will be working with the group that will be using the card catalog. Those of you in that group may raise your hand if you need help.

The students who won't be doing the assignment will be on their own. I won't have time to assist them. I'll need to give all of my time to the students who will be working on the card catalog assignment.

Divide the class into groups. If you have a card catalog that has enough drawers for half of your students, divide the class into two groups by gender. This will make it easier to see that each student participates.

Announce who will be doing the card catalog assignment today.

Assign someone to carry the 3 by 5 inch slips, the ditto pages, and the pencils to the library.

In the Library

As soon as everyone is seated, pass out the dittos and the 3 by 5 inch slips to those who will be doing the assignment.

Tell the students where they are to sit while using the card catalog drawers. Excuse five or six students at a time.

Excuse the other students to look for books.

During the period, help the students with the card catalog assignment.

Save the 3 by 5 inch slips of paper and use them for the next group(s).

FOLLOW-UP

Next week review the concepts taught in this lesson before going to the library and rotating the groups.

Classes divided into thirds for this lesson need three library visits to complete the rotation.

Name _____ Date _____

Worksheet 4.25 Card Catalog Practice

Subject _____

Author _____

Title _____

Call number _____

Go find the book on the shelves. Touch it and raise your hand. Wait until you are checked.

Name _____ Date _____

Worksheet 4.25 Card Catalog Practice

Subject _____

Author _____

Title _____

Call number _____

Go find the book on the shelves. Touch it and raise your hand. Wait until you are checked.

UNIT 5

FIFTH GRADE

What to Teach in Fifth Grade

SUGGESTIONS

1. Before your first trip to the library, refer to Appendix A, "How to Conduct Library Visits."

2. Lessons, reproducible forms, and guidelines for book reports are found in Unit 3. Written book report forms are found in Lesson 35. Oral book report guidelines are in Lesson 36. Use these materials whenever the need arises.

3. You may want to use a green (go) marker and a red (stop) marker to designate the pages you need to teach.

LESSONS

Begin by teaching Lessons 20 ("Book Care and Library Behavior") and 21 ("Appreciating Books") in Unit 3. These lessons need to be retaught each year.

If you know that your students haven't received instruction in library skills, teach Lessons 22A through 53 in Units 3 and 4. Then teach the lessons in this unit. This will bring the students up to grade level plus carry them through the lessons for the fifth grade.

If you don't know whether your students have had instruction in library skills or if you have reason to believe that they have had instruction, use Pretests 1 and 2 in Appendix B to determine subject mastery. You may want to give Pretest 1 on one day and Pretest 2 on another day. If you want to give both tests on the same day, reproduce the pretests as double-sided dittos.

If your students do poorly on Pretests 1 and 2, assume either that they have not had library instruction or that they need to have a complete reteaching of previous lessons. For bringing the students up to beginning fifth grade level, teach

Lessons 22A through 53 in Units 3 and 4. Thereafter, to cover fifth grade skills, teach the lessons in this unit.

If your students do poorly only on Pretest 2, bring them up to beginning fifth grade level by teaching Lessons 37 through 53 in Unit 4. Thereafter, to cover fifth grade skills, teach the lessons in this unit.

If your students do well on the pretests except for a couple of items, teach only the lessons related to those specific items to bring the students up to grade level. (The pretest answer page specifies the lesson in which each item was introduced.) After bringing the class up to grade level, teach the lessons in this unit to cover fifth grade skills.

If your students do well on the pretests, they are up to grade level. To cover fifth grade skills, teach the lessons in this unit.

Lesson 54. Card Catalog Review and Copyright Date

OBJECTIVES

1. To review basic catalog card instruction, which was taught in Unit 4
2. To explain the importance of the copyright date
3. To test mastery with a follow-up ditto

MATERIALS

1. A chalkboard, chalk, and eraser
2. Back-to-back reproductions of Worksheets 5.1 and 5.2

PREPARATION

Copy this catalog card on the chalkboard. Leave space between the first line and the top of the card for a line to be added.

523.3	Bronson, David
Bro	The moon; illus. by Joe Gibson.
	Williams Publishing Company 1955
	306p. illus.

LESSON

You've studied the card catalog in the past. Today we're going to review what you've learned.

How does the card catalog help you? (It tells you where you can locate specific books.)

How is the card catalog arranged? (alphabetically)

What might you know about a book that you want when you walk into a library? (author, title, or subject)

If you know the author, title, or subject, you can find the book you want if the library has it.

Look at the catalog card I've put on the chalkboard.

Ask these questions.

1. What is the title of the book? (*The Moon*)
2. Who is the author? (David Bronson)
3. Who published the book? (Williams Publishing Company)
4. What is the call number? (523.3 Bro)
5. What does "Bro" stand for? (Bronson)
6. Are there illustrations? (yes)
7. How do you know? (On the second line the card says "illus. by Joe Gibson," and on the last line it says "illus.")
8. How many pages are in the book? (306 pages)
9. Is the book fiction or nonfiction? (nonfiction)
10. How do you know? (It has a number in the left corner.)
11. What kind of card is it? (an author card)
12. How do you know? (The author's name is on the first line.)
13. What is the copyright date? (1955)

    The copyright date is particularly important for science and geography books. There are so many changes in the field of science and geography that a book about either can be quickly outdated.

    The Space Age began in 1957, two years after this book was written. In 1969 Apollo 11 landed on the moon, and firsthand exploration and study of the moon began.

    This book was written before man explored the moon. We now have much more up-to-date information. This isn't a good book to read if you want to know about the moon.

Science, geography, and history are fields that are constantly changing. If you need up-to-date information about one of these subjects, be sure to refer to a book with a recent copyright date.

Where is the copyright date located in a book? (on the back of the title page)

You don't need to be concerned about getting books with old copyrights if the subjects aren't changing much. The copyright date wouldn't be very important for a book on tigers. Information about tigers doesn't change very much.

Write the title of the book on the board inside the card, but above the author's name. (The title will appear twice on the card.)

```
                        The moon

        523.3       Bronson, David
        Bro             The moon; illus. by Joe Gibson.
                    Williams Publishing Company      1955
                        306p.    illus.
```

What kind of card is this now? (title card)

How do you know? (because the title is on the first line)

Erase the title you just added, and in its place write the subject: MOON. Be sure to write the subject in capital letters.

```
                        MOON

        523.3       Bronson, David
        Bro             The moon; illus. by Joe Gibson.
                    Williams Publishing Company      1955
                        306p.    illus.
```

What kind of card is this now? (subject card)

How do you know? (The first line is in capitals.)

We said that the card catalog helps us locate books. Look closely at this card. Can you see any other way the cards in the catalog can help us? (The cards give us information we might want to know for making reports or information we might want to know for personal reasons.)

I'm going to distribute a ditto that gives examples of three catalog cards.

Pass out the dittos.

Look at Worksheet 5.1. Notice that the three catalog cards are not a set; they are for three different books.

Ask these questions.

Author Card	Which card is an author card? (the second card) How do you know? (The author's name is on the first line.) Who is the author? (Mary Calhoun) What is the title? (*The Night the Monster Came*) What's the call number? (Fic Cal) Who is the publisher? (Morrow) Who is the illustrator? (Leslie Morrill) How many pages are in the book? (62 pages) What is the copyright date? (1982) What does "Cal" stand for? (Calhoun) What does "illus." on the last line mean? (There are illustrations—pictures—in the book.)
Title Card	Which card is a title card? (the last one) How do you know? (The title is on the first line.) Who is the author of the book? (Wilson Rawls) What is the title? (*Where the Red Fern Grows*) What's the call number? (Fic Raw) Who is the publisher? (Doubleday) Who is the illustrator? (An illustrator is not listed.) How many pages are in the book? (212 pages) What is the copyright date? (1961) What does "Raw" stand for? (Rawls)
Subject Card	Which card is a subject card? (the first card) How do you know? (The first line is in capitals.) What is the title? (*Little Black Ant*) Who is the author? (Alice Gall) Who is Fleming Crew? (co-author of the book) Who is the publisher? (Walck) What's the call number? (595.7 Gal) Who is the illustrator? (Helen Torrey) How many pages are in the book? (128 pages) What is the copyright date? (1964) What does "Gal" stand for? (Gall)

Let's see how well you understand catalog cards. Turn your papers over to Worksheet 5.2. Take out your pencils and complete the ditto.

Worksheet 5.1 The Card Catalog

ANTS

595.7 Gall, Alice
Gal   Little black ant, by Alice Gall
and Fleming Crew. Illus. by
Helen Torrey. Walck 1964
  128p. illus.

Fic Calhoun, Mary
Cal   The night the monster came.
Illus. by Leslie Morrill. Morrow
1982
  62p. illus.

Where the red fern grows

Fic Rawls, Wilson
Raw   Where the red fern grows;
the story of two dogs and a boy.
Doubleday 1961
  212p.

Worksheet 5.2 The Card Catalog

```
Nev        Neville, Emily
               It's like this, Cat; illus.
           by Emil Weiss. Harper     1963
               180p.    illus.
```

1. What is the book's title? _____

2. Who is the author? _____

3. What does "illus." on the last line mean? _____

   _____

4. What is the copyright date? _____

5. Who is the publisher? _____

6. Who is the illustrator? _____

7. How many pages are in the book? _____

8. What is the book's call number? _____

9. Is the book fiction or nonfiction? _____

10. What does "Nev" stand for? _____

Lesson 55. Card Catalog and Cross Reference Cards

OBJECTIVES

1. To introduce cross reference cards
2. To review some catalog cards

MATERIALS

1. A chalkboard, chalk, and eraser
2. Reproductions of Worksheet 5.3

PREPARATION

Copy these on the board:

```
                    Twain, Mark, pseud.

                          See

               Clemens, Samuel Langhorne



```

```
                       TRAINS

                      See also

                    RAILROADS

```

LESSON

If you look in the card catalog for Mark Twain, you might find a card that looks like this one on the board.

Point to the Mark Twain card.

Do you know what "pseud." means?

It's an abbreviation for the word *pseudonym,* which means a fictitious name, a pen name. Samuel Langhorne Clemens assumed the name Mark Twain. It was not his real name.

Some libraries file everything under an author's real name. In such libraries, if you look in the card catalog under a pseudonym, you will find a cross reference card that will direct you to the author's real name.

The card on the board is a cross reference card.

When you are using the card catalog, you have to start with what you know. If you know that you want a book by Mark Twain, look under Mark Twain's last name. If the catalog cards aren't filed under Twain, you will be directed to where they are filed.

When you find a card that directs you to look at another card, all you have to do is be obedient.

There is another kind of cross reference card. It is a "see also" card.

Perhaps you looked in the card catalog under trains. You may have found cards for several books there. You may also have found this "see also" cross reference card.

Point to the "see also" card on the board.

This card is telling you that if you need additional information, you will find some by looking under railroads.

Again, when you run into a cross reference card, all you have to do is be obedient to its direction.

You've learned a great deal about catalog cards.

I'm going to distribute a ditto which we'll do orally. Don't take your pencils out.

Distribute Worksheet 5.3.
Ask these questions.

1. What is the title of the book on Card A? (*Cowboys and Cattle Drives*)
   Card B? (*Little House on the Prairie*)
   Card C? (*Spiders*)
2. What is the author's last name on Card A? (McCall)
   Card B? (Wilder)
   Card C? (Riedman)
3. What is the call number for the book on Card A? (978 McC)
   Card B? (Fic Wil)
   Card C? (595.44 Rie)

4. Who published the book on Card A? (Childrens Press)
   Card B? (Harper)
   Card C? (Watts)

5. Who is the illustrator for the book on Card A? (Carol Rogers)
   Card B? (Garth Williams)
   Card C? (none listed)

6. How many pages are there in the book on Card A? (127 pages)
   Card B? (334 pages)
   Card C? (48 pages)

7. What is the copyright date for the book on Card A? (1964)
   Card B? (1953)
   Card C? (1979)

8. What kind of card is Card A? (subject)
   Card B? (title)
   Card C? (author)

   Very good.

Assign the students to fill in the worksheet today or at a later date, if desired.

Worksheet 5.3 The Card Catalog

COWBOYS   Card A

978   McCall, Edith
McC   Cowboys and cattle drives; illus.
         by Carol Rogers.   Childrens Press
         1964
              127p.   illus.

Little house on the prairie   Card B

Fic   Wilder, Laura Ingalls   1867–1957
Wil   Little house on the prairie;
        illus. by Garth Williams.   Harper
        1953
             334p.   illus.

595.44   Riedman, Sarah   Card C
Rie   Spiders.   Watts   1979
                48p.   illus.

Answer the following questions for each of the three cards above.

1. What is the title of each of the books?

   A. _____

   B. _____

   C. _____

2. What is the author's last name?

   A. _____ B. _____ C. _____

3. What is the call number?

   A. _____ B. _____ C. _____

4. Who is the publisher?

   A. _____ B. _____ C. _____

5. Who is the illustrator?

   A. _____ B. _____ C. _____

6. How many pages are there?

   A. _____ B. _____ C. _____

7. What is the copyright date?

   A. _____ B. _____ C. _____

8. What kind of card is each?

   A. _____ B. _____ C. _____

Lesson 56. Card Catalog and Special Cards

OBJECTIVES

1. To introduce an illustrator card
2. To introduce a subject analytic card
3. To introduce an annotated card

MATERIAL

Reproductions of Worksheet 5.4

LESSON

You've learned a great deal about catalog cards. Today you're going to learn some new things.

I'm going to distribute a ditto. As soon as you receive your copy, study the first card and see if you can determine what kind of card it is.

Distribute the ditto.

Look at the first card.

Does anyone know what kind of card it is? (an illustrator card)

See the abbreviation "illus." on the first line. "Illus." stands for illustrator.

What is an illustrator? (a person who creates the pictures for a book)

You remember that most books have three catalog cards: an author card, a title card, and a subject card.

If an illustrator is important to a book, often a card is made for that illustrator.

Some books have four cards: an author card, a title card, a subject card, and an illustrator card.

Look at the illustrator card.

Who is the illustrator? (Susan Jeffers)

Who is the author? (Robert Frost)

What are the dates after Robert Frost's name? (1874–1963, the dates of his birth and his death)

What is the title of the book? (*Stopping by Woods on a Snowy Evening*)

You'll notice that the title is not capitalized like you capitalize. Librarians capitalize only the first words and proper names in titles.

Look at the second card.

Ask these questions.

1. What kind of card is it? (a subject card)
2. How do you know? (The first line is completely capitalized.)
3. Do you think the whole book is about the subject Amelia Earhart? (no, only pages 117–146)

This card is called a *subject analytic card*. It refers to a subject that is just a part of a book.

Look at the third card.

The author is Eric Mowbray Knight, who was born in 1897 and died in 1943. The title of the book is *Lassie Come-Home*. The book was illustrated by Don Bolognese. This is a revised edition. Revised means the book has been corrected, improved, or brought up to date. Holt, Rinehart and Winston published the book.

Notice that there are two dates. The book was copyrighted in 1940, but this revised edition came out in 1971.

There are 230 pages and there are illustrations in the book.

The information after that is a description of the book. It's called an *annotation*. It can help you decide whether this is a book you'd like to read.

I'll read the annotation to you. "To meet her former owner, a collie undertakes a thousand-mile journey."

This book is considered by many to be the greatest dog book ever written.

Look at the three cards.

Which card is a subject analytic card? (the second one)

Which card is an illustrator card? (the first one)

Which card has an annotation—a description of the book's contents? (the last one)

You did a good job.

Pass the dittos in.

Worksheet 5.4 The Card Catalog

Jeffers, Susan, illus

811.52   Frost, Robert, 1874–1963
Fro   Stopping by woods on a snowy
evening, by Robert Frost.   Illus.
by Susan Jeffers.   Dutton   1978
              32p.   illus.

EARHART, AMELIA, pages 117–146

920   Nathan, Dorothy
Nat   Women of courage;   illus. by
Carolyn Cather.   Random House   1964
              188p.   illus.

Kni   Knight, Eric Mowbray, 1897–1943
                  Lassie come-home. Illus. by Don
Bolognese.   (Revised edition)
Holt, Rinehart and Winston   (1971,
c. 1940)
                  230p.   illus.

To meet her former owner, a
collie undertakes a thousand-
mile journey.

Lesson 57. Card Catalog Practice in the Library

OBJECTIVES

1. To teach students how to distinguish between nonfiction and fiction catalog cards
2. To give students practice using the card catalog

MATERIALS

1. A chalkboard, chalk, and eraser
2. Reproductions of Worksheet 5.5
3. A card catalog

PREPARATIONS

1. Copy these two catalog cards on the board.

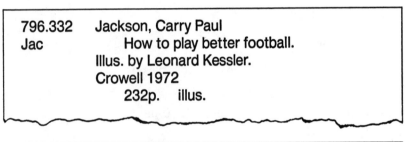

```
796.332   Jackson, Carry Paul
Jac              How to play better football.
          Illus. by Leonard Kessler.
          Crowell 1972
                232p.   illus.
```

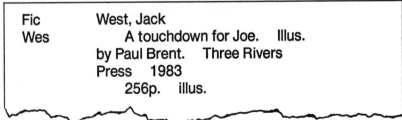

```
Fic       West, Jack
Wes              A touchdown for Joe.    Illus.
          by Paul Brent.    Three Rivers
          Press    1983
                256p.   illus.
```

2. Schedule a library visit.

LESSON

Present this lesson immediately before your scheduled library visit.

I've put two catalog cards on the board.

Point to the card for *How to Play Better Football*.

Look at this one first.

Ask these questions.

1. What is the title of the book? (*How to Play Better Football*)
2. Who illustrated it? (Leonard Kessler)
3. What is the copyright date? (1972)
4. How many pages are in the book? (232 pages)
5. Who is the author? (Carry Paul Jackson)
6. Who is the publisher? (Crowell)
7. What does "illus." on the last line mean? (There are illustrations—pictures—in the book.)
8. What is the call number? (796.332 Jac)
9. What does "Jac" stand for? (Jackson)
10. Is the book fiction or nonfiction? (nonfiction)
11. How do you know? (Nonfiction books have numbers in the left corner.)
12. What kind of card is it? (an author card)

Point to the card for *A Touchdown for Joe.*

Look at this card.

Ask these questions.

1. Who is the author of the book? (Jack West)
2. What is the title? (*A Touchdown for Joe*)
3. How many pages are in the book? (256 pages)
4. Who illustrated it? (Paul Brent)
5. Who is the publisher? (Three Rivers Press)
6. What is the copyright date? (1983)
7. What is the call number? (Fic Wes)
8. What does "illus." on the last line mean? (There are illustrations—pictures—in the book.)
9. Is the book fiction or nonfiction? (fiction)
10. How do you know? (Nonfiction books have numbers. Fiction books don't have numbers. "Fic" means fiction.)

Point to the card for *How to Play Better Football.*

Look again at the card for *How to Play Better Football.* How do you know that the book is nonfiction? (It has a number in the left corner.)

Look again at the card for *A Touchdown for Joe.* How do you know it's fiction? (It doesn't have a number.)

I'm going to distribute a ditto. Don't put your name on it yet. Read it.

Distribute the papers.

Notice that the top half of the paper tells you how to determine whether a book is nonfiction or fiction.

We're going to the library today. When we get there, half of you will do this assignment paper. The other half will browse and check out books. The next time we go to the library, the two groups will rotate.

When we get to the library, those who are going to do the assignment today will be given a drawer from the card catalog. They are to look through the drawer, select a subject, and find a nonfiction and a fiction card for that subject.

Notice that there is a line where the subject should be written. The following lines are for recording information about a nonfiction and a fiction title.

Those who are going to do the assignment may check out books if they finish their papers before the period is over.

Today the girls (or boys) will do the assignment.

If you're not going to be doing the assignment today, pass your papers in.

If your students need to take their pencils to the library, remind them of this fact. Remind the students who are going to do the assignment to take their papers with them.

At the Library

1. Have the class enter the library in two groups: those who will be doing the assignment and those who will be checking books out.

2. Everyone should be seated with his or her own group after entering the library.

3. Excuse a few of the students who have assignments to get card catalog drawers. Have them take the drawers to their tables. Continue excusing the students in the assignment group until they all have gotten drawers.

4. Excuse the group that will be browsing and checking out books.

5. Circulate among those doing the assignment. Check the papers as you walk around to see if the students are on the right track. Help students who need assistance.

6. Students who finish their assignments early should give their papers to you and then check out a book.

7. If possible, when a student hands his or her paper to you, grade, discuss, and return it on the spot.

FOLLOW-UP

Next week review the concepts taught in this lesson before going to the library and rotating the groups.

Worksheet 5.5 The Card Catalog

To identify a fiction or nonfiction book, look at the left-hand corner of the catalog card. If there is a number in the left-hand corner, the book is nonfiction.

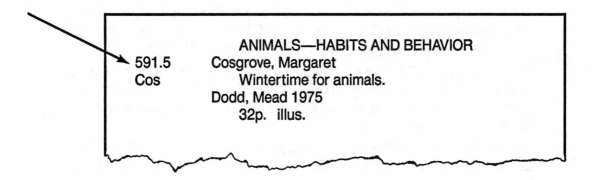

ANIMALS—HABITS AND BEHAVIOR
591.5   Cosgrove, Margaret
Cos   Wintertime for animals.
         Dodd, Mead 1975
              32p. illus.

If there isn't a number in the left-hand corner, the book is fiction.

ANIMALS—FICTION

Law   Lawson, Robert, 1892–1957
              Rabbit Hill. Viking Press 1944
              127p. illus.

Subject _____

<u>Nonfiction</u>

    Title _____

    Author _____

    Call Number _____

<u>Fiction</u>

    Title _____

    Author _____

    Call Number _____

Lesson 58. Introducing Encyclopedias

OBJECTIVES

1. To introduce encyclopedias
2. To teach students about encyclopedia arrangement, guide words, cross references, headings, maps, authors, and so forth.
3. To present dittos showing a one-volume encyclopedia, sets of encyclopedias, and encyclopedia articles

MATERIALS

1. Back-to-back reproductions of Worksheets 5.6 and 5.7
2. Back-to-back reproductions of Worksheets 5.8 and 5.9
3. A set of encyclopedias displayed in the front of the room (if available)

LESSON

Today we are going to talk about encyclopedias.

Basically there are two kinds of encyclopedias. First, there's the kind that gives you information on all branches of knowledge. That means the encyclopedia covers everything—science, history, religion, art, sports, and so forth. Some examples of this type are *The World Book Encyclopedia, Compton's Encyclopedia,* and *Britannica Junior.*

Second, there's the kind that gives information about only one field of knowledge. That means the encyclopedia covers only one subject. Some examples are *The Encyclopedia of Dogs, The Encyclopedia of Motorcycling,* and *The Encyclopedia of American Music.*

An encyclopedia can be one book or a set of books. *The Baseball Encyclopedia* is one book. *The World Book Encyclopedia* is a set of books.

There can be a set of encyclopedias on one subject, such as art.

Encyclopedias are reference books. Reference books are not designed to be read from cover to cover. One usually goes to a reference book for quick information or to find brief coverage of a subject.

Encyclopedias have articles about important people, places, things, and happenings.

Some of the articles are one paragraph long; some are many pages long.

Encyclopedias are usually arranged alphabetically.

Dictionaries deal with words. Encyclopedias are different: they deal with subjects.

If You Have a Set of Encyclopedias

1. Point to them.
2. Give the name of the set.
3. Hold up a volume and tell the students that this is a volume.
4. Define the word *volume.* (A *volume* is one of the books in a set. The word *volume* also means a single book complete in itself.)
5. Tell how many volumes are in the set.
6. Tell which volume the index is in.

I'm going to distribute a double-sided ditto that gives some examples of encyclopedias. Read and study both sides.

Distribute reproductions of Worksheets 5.6 and 5.7.
Give the students time to read and study the ditto.

Look at Worksheet 5.6.

The twenty-two-volume set you see pictured on this page covers all branches of knowledge.

Look at Volumes 3 and 4. There were so many articles on subjects beginning with the letter "C" that two volumes were required to hold them. Articles from "C" to "Ch" can be found in Volume 3, and articles from "Ci" to "Cz" can be found in Volume 4.

Look at Volume 11. There weren't many articles starting with the letters "J" and "K," so the articles were combined in one volume.

Look at Volume 21. There weren't many articles beginning with "W," "X," "Y," and "Z," so the four letters were put in one volume.

In which volume would you look for information about snakes? (Volume 17, S–Sn)

Camping? (Volume 3, C–Ch)

Yankee Doodle? (Volume 21, W–X–Y–Z)

Generally speaking, people are listed in encyclopedias by their last names.

In which volume would you look for an article about Susan B. Anthony? (Volume 1, A)

Davy Crockett? (Volume 4, Ci–Cz)

Annie Oakley? (Volume 14, N–O)

Johnny Appleseed? (Volume 1, A)

Kings and queens are entered in encyclopedias differently. To find an article about Queen Elizabeth, look in Volume 6, E.

In which volume would you look for an article about King Henry VIII? (Volume 9, H)

Queen Victoria? (Volume 20, U–V)

You've learned how to find kings, queens, and other people in an encyclopedia. For most other subjects you should look under the *first* word. For example, if you want to find sand dollar, look in Volume 17, S–Sn.

In which volume would you look for the Statue of Liberty? (Volume 18, So–Sz)

Tropical rain forest? (Volume 19, T)

Dude ranch? (Volume 5, D)

Turn the ditto over.

An encyclopedia can be one book. A one-volume encyclopedia can cover all subjects, like the first book pictured, or it can cover only one subject like the last three books.

I'm going to pass out a double-sided ditto that shows two pages from *The World Book Encyclopedia,* which is a twenty-two-volume set.

Distribute reproductions of Worksheets 5.8 and 5.9.

Encyclopedias have guide words at the top of the pages just like dictionaries. The guide words help you to locate the article you are seeking.

Look at Worksheet 5.8.

Notice the alphabetical guide at the top left: log cabin. The other guide would be on the facing page at the top right.

This page on log cabin is an example of a short article.

Let's count the number of paragraphs. The first paragraph starts with: "Log Cabin. The first English colonists . . . "

The next paragraph starts with: "The log cabin was not easy to build . . . "

The next one starts: "Many noted Americans . . . "

We have found three paragraphs.

Note the additional material at the end of the article. That material starts out: "See also." "See also" is a cross reference term. It means if you want more information related to this subject, you may also look under the articles that are listed there.

Let's look at the cross references. Follow me.

If you look under PIONEER LIFE IN AMERICA, you'll find information about a pioneer home.

If you look under COLONIAL LIFE IN AMERICA, you'll find information about houses.

If you look under BUCHANAN, JAMES, you'll find a picture.

If you look under KENTUCKY, you'll find a picture of Lincoln's birthplace.

Are all of these cross references in the same volume as log cabin (in Volume L)? (no)

In which volume would you find PIONEER LIFE IN AMERICA in the encyclopedia shown on Worksheet 5.6? (Volume 15, P, on Worksheet 5.6)

COLONIAL LIFE IN AMERICA? (Volume 4, Ci–Cz, on Worksheet 5.6)

BUCHANAN, JAMES? (Volume 2, B, on Worksheet 5.6)

KENTUCKY? (Volume 11, J–K, on Worksheet 5.6)

Look at the end of the third paragraph. See the name Walker D. Wyman.

Walker D. Wyman is the one who wrote the article on Log Cabin.

The next subject is LOG-CABIN AND HARD-CIDER CAMPAIGN.

Is there an article there? (no)

What do we have? (a cross reference)

We are told to look under HARRISON, WILLIAM H. for information about the log-cabin and hard-cider campaign.

In which volume should we look? (Volume 9, H, on Worksheet 5.6)

Look at the next entry: LOGAN.

See the parentheses, the dates, and the question marks.

What do you think the dates and question marks mean? (As far as can be determined, Logan was born in 1725 and died in 1786. The question marks mean that the dates are not certain.)

Turn your dittos over to Worksheet 5.9.

This article is about Lapland. Notice that the subject LAPLAND is followed by its pronunciation. The large *LAP* means the emphasis is on "LAP." "Land" is not emphasized.

As you glance at the article, you notice that some words are in dark black type. These are called *main heads,* short for *main headings.* Some articles have subheads, too, which are used to subdivide the information under main headings.

I'm going to read the main headings to you. Follow on your paper.

Location and Size
The Land and Its Resources
The People
Language and Religion
Work of the People
History

How do you think these main headings can help you? (By glancing at the main headings, you can quickly locate the information you want.)

Find the main heading Language and Religion. Look at the second paragraph. I'm going to read the first two sentences. Follow on your paper.

Read the two sentences. (All Lapps once believed in a form of magic called *shamanism*. The *shaman* (medicine man) beats drums to foretell the future (see SHAMAN).

What is a *shaman?* (a medicine man)

There's a cross reference in the second sentence. Where are we told to look? (under SHAMAN)

Would SHAMAN be in the same volume of the encyclopedia as Lapland? (no, in an S volume, *or,* if referring to Worksheet 5.6, in Volume 17, S–Sn)

Look at the end of the article. There's a name: John H. Wuorinen. Who is he? (the author of the article)

At the end of the article we have three cross references. Who can read them? (SWEDEN, CLOTHING, EUROPE)

What are these cross references for? (to direct you to other articles related to Lapland.)

Look at the map. Lapland is the dark area.

See the scale of miles at the lower right. About three-quarters of an inch is equal to 500 miles.

About how far is it to Helsinki from the southern edge of Lapland? (about 400 miles)

About how far is it from the southern edge of Lapland to Poland? (about 900 miles)

You did a good job.

Collect the dittos.

Worksheet 5.6 Encyclopedias

A	B	C-Ch	Ci-Cz	D	E	F	G	H	I	J-K	L	M	N-O	P	Q-R	S-Sn	So-Sz	T	U-V	W-X Y-Z	Research Guide and Index
1	2	3	4	5	6	7	8	9	10	11	12	13	14	15	16	17	18	19	20	21	22

Pictured above is a set of encyclopedias containing twenty-two volumes. Some sets of encyclopedias cover all fields of knowledge: science, history, religion, art, sports, and so forth. Some examples are *The World Book Encyclopedia, Compton's Encyclopedia,* and *Britannica Junior.* Other sets of encyclopedias give information on only one field of knowledge. Some examples are *Science Encyclopedia, The Encyclopedia of Art,* and *The Folk Song Encyclopedia.*

Worksheet 5.7 One-Volume Encyclopedias

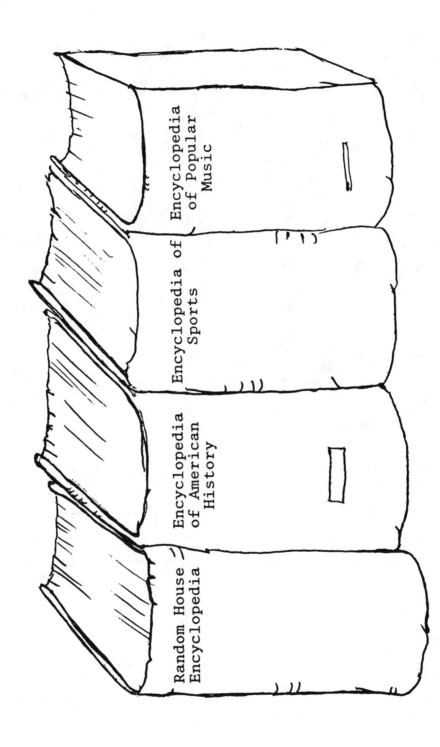

Pictured above are some examples of one-volume encyclopedias. The first book covers all branches of knowledge—all subjects. The other three encyclopedias cover one subject each.

Worksheet 5.8 Encyclopedia Article

LOG CABIN

Fireplace Frame

Chinking Between Logs

Fitted Notches

Notching and Hewing

Splitting Log

American Pioneers Built Log Cabins entirely from the materials available in the wilderness. With their simple tools, they shaped, split, and notched logs to make these sturdy shelters. Log cabins served as both homes and fortresses on the frontier.

LOG CABIN. The first English colonists in North America did not know how to build houses of logs. They lived in shelters made of brush and bark until they could erect frame houses like those they had known in England. But colonists who had lived in the forests of Switzerland, Germany, and Scandinavia knew how to build log houses. Swedish settlers who came to Delaware in 1638 built the first log cabins in America. German pioneers who settled in Pennsylvania built the first log cabins there about 1710. But Scotch-Irish immigrants made the first wide use of logs when they moved to the "back country" of the Appalachian highlands after 1720. By the time of the American Revolutionary War, settlers along the whole western frontier were using log cabins.

The log cabin was not easy to build, although it required few tools. Builders used three types of logs: round, hewn on two sides, and squared. The logs had to be about the same size so that the cracks between them could be easily *chinked* (filled) with moss, clay, or mud. Builders had to be careful in cutting the notches where the logs fitted together. They usually covered the cabin roof with bark or thatch, and later with rough wooden shingles cut from logs. Most log cabins

did not have windows, because few people could afford glass panes. But settlers often covered openings with animal skins or greased paper. They made doors and floors from logs split lengthwise. The door was usually hung on leather hinges. Most log cabins had one story, with one or two rooms. Some had a loft for sleeping and storage, which people could reach with a ladder, or by steps cut into the cabin wall. Later, pioneers erected two-story log houses with several rooms.

Many noted Americans, including Abraham Lincoln, were born in log cabins. To rise from such humble beginnings to become President has long been part of the American dream of equality and opportunity. The log cabin came to symbolize the dream of being able to improve one's place in life.   WALKER D. WYMAN

See also PIONEER LIFE IN AMERICA (A Pioneer Home); COLONIAL LIFE IN AMERICA (Houses); BUCHANAN, JAMES (picture); KENTUCKY (picture: Lincoln Birthplace).

LOG-CABIN AND HARD-CIDER CAMPAIGN. See HARRISON, WILLIAM H. (Elections of 1836 and 1840).

LOGAN (1725?-1786?), a Cayuga Indian chief, won fame for a stirring speech in 1774. White settlers along the Ohio River had murdered some Indians, including

Worksheet 5.9 Encyclopedia Article

LAPLAND, *LAP land,* lies in the extreme northern part of Europe, above the Arctic Circle. The region is called Lapland because it is the home of a small, sturdy people known as the Lapps. But it does not form a separate country. The region that makes up Lapland belongs to Norway, Sweden, Finland, and Russia.

Lapland has a cold climate. Winter lasts nine months every year. The other three months resemble spring in areas that have mild climates. Because Lapland lies so far north, it has a period of two months in summer when the sky never darkens. The sun never rises above the horizon for two months each winter.

Location and Size. Lapland covers about 150,000 square miles (388,000 square kilometers). It stretches across the northern parts of Norway, Sweden, Finland, and Russia. The region includes all of northern Norway, the Swedish province of Norrbotten and part of Norrland, all of northern Finland, and the Kola Peninsula of Russia (see EUROPE [color map]). Lapland has no

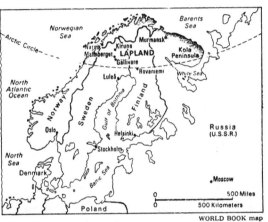

Location of Lapland

definite boundary to the south. The Norwegian, Barents, and White seas lie to the north.

The Land and Its Resources. Lapland is a bleak, barren region with few trees and thin, stunted vegetation. Of the trees, only birches, pines, and firs manage to survive. But they are only midget trees, kept small by the cold climate. Plant life consists primarily of mosses and lichens. Many reindeer feed on the scanty vegetation. Some wander wild, but the people herd many reindeer like cattle. The reindeer are an important source of food and serve as draft and pack animals.

Iron and nickel provide the most valuable mineral resources. Beds of iron lie deep under the soil of southern Swedish Lapland. The nickel deposits are in the Russian part of the region. Lapland's iron deposits rank among the largest in the world. The iron mines at Gällivare, Kiruna, and Malmberget are some of the world's richest. A railroad links the iron fields with Luleå, on the Gulf of Bothnia, and another connects with Narvik, Norway. The railroads carry iron ore to these ports for export to other countries.

The People. Lapland has a population of about 34,000. About 2,500 of the people live in Finland, 10,000 in Sweden, 20,000 in Norway, and 1,500 in Russia. The Lapps are among the smallest peoples of Europe.

They average only about 5 feet (150 centimeters) in height, but are strong and muscular. Lapps look somewhat like Chinese or Japanese. They have low foreheads, high cheekbones, straight black hair, and slightly yellowish skin. Their noses are often broad and flat, and their lips are straight and thin. Some Lapps live outside Lapland, in central Sweden and Finland and in Norway. Many have married Swedes, Finns, or Norwegians, and their physical type is changing.

The Lapps are mostly a nomadic people who follow reindeer herds. But many have settled in fishing or farming villages. They dress in clothes made of wool and reindeer skins. Their everyday garments are so colorful that they resemble holiday costumes. The Lapps are healthy and happy, although they must work hard to live in their bleak land.

Language and Religion. The language of Lapland is related to that spoken in Finland. The people in various sections speak sharply different dialects. Many Lapps have no formal education, because there are few schools.

All Lapps once believed in a form of magic called *shamanism.* The *shaman* (medicine man) beats drums to foretell the future (see SHAMAN). Today, most Lapps belong to the Lutheran or Eastern Orthodox churches. The people often have trouble attending church because they live so far away. But they will cross vast distances to attend church when they are to be married or wish to bury their dead.

Work of the People. The Lapps may be grouped according to their primary means of livelihood. These groups are: (1) the Mountain Lapps, (2) the Sea Lapps, and (3) the River Lapps.

Mountain Lapps live a wandering life. They move from one place to another with their herds of reindeer. These nomads pitch their tents wherever there is enough vegetation to feed the herds. An entire family lives in a single cone-shaped tent, shared by the family dogs. The Mountain Lapps live chiefly on reindeer meat, milk, and cheese.

Sea Lapps live along the coast in huts made of wood and covered with sod. They earn their livelihood primarily by fishing. The Sea Lapps are more civilized than the Mountain Lapps. The Sea Lapps often build their huts in groups to form fishing communities.

River Lapps live in settlements along the river banks. They are the most progressive people in Lapland. They have a kind of community life, and occasionally do a little farming. The River Lapps fish and hunt, and keep herds of reindeer, cattle, and sheep.

History. Anthropologists believe that the Lapps moved to Lapland from central Asia thousands of years ago. Finnish merchants began to trade with the Lapps in the 1300's. Swedish kings held the title "King of the Lapps" in the 1500's and 1600's. But the people have always lived about the same way as they do today, with only loose community organization and little government control.   JOHN H. WUORINEN

See also SWEDEN (People); CLOTHING (picture: Lapp Family); EUROPE (picture: Reindeer).

Lesson 59. Encyclopedia Indexes and Study Aids

OBJECTIVES

1. To teach students how to use an encyclopedia index
2. To present an example of the study aid material that can be found at the end of some articles

MATERIALS

1. Back-to-back reproductions of Worksheets 5.10 and 5.11
2. A chalkboard, chalk, and eraser

LESSON

If you want to find some information in an encyclopedia, you may look directly under the subject you have in mind. For example, if you want some information about bicycles, you may get the "B" Volume and look under BICYCLE.

Another way to find information is to use the encyclopedia's index.

Sometimes sets of encyclopedias have their indexes in their last volume. For example, *The World Book Encyclopedia* has its index in Volume 22 of its twenty-two-volume set.

Some subjects can be found within other articles. For example, if you wanted to find some information about Princess Diana, you would soon discover that you couldn't find an article under Diana in the "D" Volume. However, if you looked in the index volume under Diana, you would be referred to an article on Prince Charles and an article on Queen Elizabeth. Both of these articles have information about Princess Diana.

The index volume can help you find information that you can't find by looking directly under the subject.

I'm going to distribute a double-sided ditto.

Distribute the ditto.

Look at Worksheet 5.10, which is a reprint from *The World Book Encyclopedia*.

Notice the guide words at the top left: Péligot, Eugène. On the facing page of the index volume there is another guide word.

Who remembers how guide words help you? (They tell you whether the subject you are looking for will be found between the guide words on the facing pages.)

Notice that there are three columns on the page.

Hold up a copy of the ditto. Point to each of the three columns.

Find *penguin* on this index page.

Check to see that everyone has found it.

Actually there are five entries for penguin or penguins. Look at the dark type. Follow with your finger as I read the entries:

Penguin
Penguin
Penguin Books
Penguin Island
Penguins, Pittsburgh

Let's say that we want to find information about an animal called *penguin.* Which of those five entries do we want? (the first)

How do you know? (The word *bird* in parentheses after *penguin* means that the information will be about an animal.)

What is the second penguin? (a boat)

What is the third entry? (Penguin Books, which is a publishing company)

What is the fourth entry? (the name of a book)

After the entry *Penguin Island,* we read: "book by France." Do you think the country of France wrote the book? (no)

Then why does it say France? (An author named Anatole France wrote the book.)

What information are you given about the last entry: Penguins, Pittsburgh? (The Pittsburgh Penguins is a hockey team.)

Let's look back at the first entry. I'm going to put part of it on the board.

Copy this on the board:

Penguin . . .
    Animal . . .
    Antarctica . . .
    Bird . . .
    Life . . .

Look at the board. What do the periods mean? (I didn't write everything; there is more.)

Look at the first penguin entry on your ditto. It's a main heading in dark black letters.

Who can tell me what information you can get from the first line? (We are talking about a bird named penguin. For information, look in the "P" Volume, page 212. The article has pictures.)

The lines under Penguin are indented. They are subheads. The subheads will lead you to other information.

Add "Main head" and "Subheads" plus connecting lines to your board example.

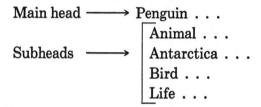

Point as you explain the following.

Penguin is the main head—the main heading. Animal, Antarctica, Bird, and Life are the subheads.

Look back at your paper. Who can explain the line under Penguin—the first subhead? (In the article on ANIMAL in the "A" Volume, page 460, there is a picture of a penguin.)

Who can explain the next subhead? (In the article ANTARCTICA, under the heading of Birds, "A" Volume, page 499, you will find information and pictures.)

Who can explain the next subhead? (In the article on BIRD under the heading Birds of the Ocean and the Antarctic, "B" Volume, page 266, you will find information and a picture.)

Who can explain the last subhead? (In the article on LIFE under The Physical Environment, "L" Volume, page 242a, you will find information with a picture.)

Sometimes when a publisher prepares a new edition of an encyclopedia, new material is added. To keep the page numbers somewhat the same as those of the last edition, the same page number may be used several times. Differentiation is made possible by adding letters to the page numbers. For example, pages could be added between 242 and 243 by numbering them 242a, 242b, 242c, and so forth. An *edition* means the copies printed and issued at or near the same time. If material is added to an encyclopedia before printing copies the next time, it is a new edition.

Turn your ditto over.

At the end of some articles you'll find study aids. This page of study aids is found at the end of a twenty-four-page article on insects.

Look at the first main heading: Related Articles. Put your finger on it. I'll read what it says. (Read: See BEETLE; FLY; and MOTH with their lists of Related Articles. See also the following articles.)

It instructs you to look under BEETLE, FLY, and MOTH. Those articles have lists of Related Articles, which may be of help, too. Then you can look at the articles listed below under the headings Other Insects, Life Changes, and Other Related Articles.

Keep your finger on the main head: Related Articles. How many subheads are there? (3)

Who wants to read the subheads? (Other Insects, Life Changes, Other Related Articles)

Put your finger on the first subhead—Other Insects. See that long list of insects under it? You can find an article on every one of those insects in this set of encyclopedias.

Put your finger on the second subhead—Life Changes. There are eight life changes listed. There are articles on each of them.

Put your finger on the third subhead—Other Related Articles. There are some more related subjects for which you can find articles.

Next is an outline, which gives you an overall view of the article.

Then there's a list of questions, which help you review important information.

And last, under Additional Resources, you see a list of books about insects. This list is divided into two parts: Level I and Level II. Level I books are easier to read than the Level II books. If you want to read some books about insects, you might read some from these lists.

Look at the first entry under Level I. Put your finger on it.

It reads: Anderson, Margaret J. *Exploring the Insect World*, McGraw, 1974.

Margaret J. Anderson is the author of a book titled *Exploring the Insect World*.

Notice the different kind of type with which *Exploring the Insect World* is printed? It's called *italic type*. One of its uses is to designate titles of books.

McGraw is the publisher.

1974 is the copyright date.

You've learned a great deal about encyclopedias. You should be able to use them quite well now.

Collect the dittos.

Worksheet 5.10 Encyclopedia Index

Worksheet 5.11 Encyclopedia Study Aids

INSECT / *Study Aids*

Related Articles. See BEETLE; FLY; and MOTH with their lists of Related Articles. See also the following articles:

OTHER INSECTS

Ant	Leafhopper
Ant Lion	Locust
Aphid	Louse
Bedbug	Mantid
Bee	Mayfly
Bug	Mole Cricket
Bumblebee	Mormon Cricket
Butterfly	Phylloxera
Chinch Bug	San Jose Scale
Cicada	Sawfly
Cockroach	Scale Insect
Cricket	Scorpion Fly
Dragonfly	Silver Fish
Earwig	Stinkbug
Flea	Stone Fly
Grasshopper	Termite
Hellgrammite	Thrips
Hornet	Walking Stick
Ichneumon Fly	Wasp
Katydid	Water Bug
Lacewing	Yellow Jacket
Leaf Insect	

LIFE CHANGES

Caterpillar	Grub	Metamorphosis
Chrysalis	Larva	Pupa
Cocoon	Maggot	

OTHER RELATED ARTICLES

Animal	Insecticide
Antarctica (Land Animals)	Linnaeus, Carolus
Arthropod	Mimicry
Bioluminescence	Molting
Bird (The Importance of Birds)	Parasite (Animal Parasites; pictures)
Classification, Scientific	Pheromone
Compound Eye	Plant (Insect-Eating Plants)
Disease (Spread of Infectious Diseases)	Pollen and Pollination
Entomology	Protective Coloration
Forestry	Swammerdam, Jan
Frisch, Karl von	Virus (How Viruses Are Used)
Gardening (Caring for the Garden)	

Outline

I. The World of Insects
  A. The Variety of Insects
  B. Why Insects Have Survived
II. The Importance of Insects
  A. Beneficial Insects
  B. Harmful Insects
  C. Insect Control
III. The Bodies of Insects
  A. Skeleton
  B. Head
  C. Thorax
  D. Abdomen
  E. Internal Organs
IV. The Senses of Insects
  A. Sight
  B. Hearing
  C. Touch
  D. Taste
  E. Smell
V. The Life Cycle of Insects
  A. Reproduction
  B. Growth and Development
VI. The Ways of Life of Insects
  A. Courtship
  B. Family Life
  C. Hibernation and Migration
  D. Protection from Enemies
  E. Why Insects Behave As They Do
VII. The Orders of Insects

Questions

What body features do all species of insects have in common?

Why can many insects walk and lay eggs even though their heads have been cut off?

How long do most adult insects live?

What are some ways in which insects are beneficial and harmful to human beings?

Why does a growing insect shed its exoskeleton?

Which insects are probably the fastest fliers? How fast can they fly?

How do insects hear? How do they make sounds?

What are some ways in which insects protect themselves from their enemies?

How do spiders differ from insects?

What are some reasons for the success of insects in their struggle for survival?

What are the three patterns of insect growth and development? How do they differ?

Additional Resources

Level I

ANDERSON, MARGARET J. *Exploring the Insect World.* McGraw, 1974.

CHENG, LANNA, ed. *Marine Insects.* Elsevier, 1976.

CONKLIN, GLADYS P. *How Insects Grow.* Holiday, 1969. *Insects Build Their Homes.* 1972.

FIELDS, ALICE. *Insects.* Watts, 1980.

HOGNER, DOROTHY C. *Good Bugs and Bad Bugs in Your Garden: Back-Yard Ecology.* Harper, 1974.

HUTCHINS, ROSS E. *The Bug Clan.* Dodd, 1973. *Insects and Their Young.* 1975.

LIGHTNER, ALICE M. *Bugs—Big and Little.* Simon & Schuster, 1980.

PATENT, DOROTHY H. *How Insects Communicate.* Holiday, 1975. *Plants and Insects Together.* 1976.

SELSAM, MILLICENT E., and HUNT, JOYCE. *A First Look at Insects.* Walker, 1975.

TEALE, EDWIN W. *The Strange Lives of Familiar Insects.* Dodd, 1962. *The Junior Book of Insects.* 2nd ed. Dutton, 1972.

Level II

BORROR, DONALD J., and WHITE, R. E. *A Field Guide to the Insects of America North of Mexico.* Houghton, 1970.

BORROR, DONALD J., and DELONG, D. M. *An Introduction to the Study of Insects.* 3rd ed. Holt, 1971.

CALLAHAN, PHILIP S. *Insect Behavior.* Four Winds, 1970. *Insects and How They Function.* Holiday House, 1971.

COMSTOCK, JOHN H. *An Introduction to Entomology.* 9th ed. Comstock, 1940.

FABRE, JEAN H. C. *Social Life in the Insect World.* Gale, 1974. Reprint of 1914 ed. *Insects.* Scribner, 1979.

GRZIMEK, BERNHARD, ed. *Grzimek's Animal Life Encyclopedia: Volume 2, Insects.* Van Nostrand, 1975.

JOHNSON, WARREN T., and LYON, H. H. *Insects That Feed on Trees and Shrubs: An Illustrated Practical Guide.* Comstock, 1976.

LINSENMAIER, WALTER. *Insects of the World.* McGraw, 1972.

LUTZ, FRANK E. *Field Book of Insects of the United States and Canada.* Rev. ed. Putnam, 1948.

MALLIS, ARNOLD. *American Entomologists.* Rutgers, 1971.

MILNE, LORUS J. and MARGERY. *The Audubon Society Field Guide to North American Insects and Spiders.* Knopf, 1980. *Insect Worlds: A Guide for Man on Making the Most of the Environment.* Scribner, 1980.

SWAN, LESTER A., and PAPP, C. S. *The Common Insects of North America.* Harper, 1972.

TWEEDIE, MICHAEL W. F. *Atlas of Insects.* Harper, 1974. *Insect Life.* Taplinger, 1977.

WILSON, EDWARD O. *The Insect Societies.* Harvard, 1971.

Lesson 60. Encyclopedia Review

OBJECTIVES

1. To review encyclopedias
2. To teach students about some special features found in encyclopedias
3. To administer a follow-up ditto

MATERIALS

1. A chalkboard, chalk, and eraser
2. Back-to-back reproductions of Worksheets 5.12 and 5.13
3. If desired, reproductions of Worksheet 5.14

LESSON

We've been studying about encyclopedias. Let's see what you remember.

Encyclopedias differ in their coverage. Who can explain that difference? (Some encyclopedias cover all fields of knowledge. Others cover only one field of knowledge.)

Encyclopedias also differ in their length. Who can explain that difference? (Some encyclopedias are one volume long. Others are sets of varying length.)

How are encyclopedias usually arranged? (alphabetically)

If a set of encyclopedias has one volume for each letter of the alphabet, in which volume would you look for an article about whales? ("W" Volume)

Lightning? ("L" Volume)

Eskimos? ("E" Volume)

Do encyclopedias have guide words? (yes)

What is the purpose of guide words? (They tell you whether the subject you are seeking will be found between the guide words on the facing pages.)

Sometimes when you are reading an encyclopedia article you are directed to look under a different subject. What is such a direction called? (a cross reference)

Write this on the board: (1620?–1683?)

Sometimes when you look a person up in an encyclopedia, you see something like this after his or her name. What does it mean? (The dates represent the dates the subject was born and died. The question marks mean the dates are not certain.)

You can find information about a subject by looking directly in an encyclopedia under that subject. What is another way you can find information? (Use the encyclopedia's index.)

Encyclopedias often have special features. I'm going to pass out a ditto that gives you some examples.

Distribute back-to-back reproductions of Worksheets 5.12 and 5.13.

Look at Worksheet 5.12.

Point to the first feature pictured on the page. See the arrow pointing to the name.

Michael E. DeBakey is the author of the article. Authors sign the articles they write. If you want to know something about the author, you can look in the "A" Volume where there's information about contributors.

Put your finger on the second feature—Facts in Brief. Here you are looking at a table of facts about Texas. You can see at a glance that the capital is Austin.

Read the other information in the table to the students.

Put your finger on the third special feature. When specialized subjects are discussed, tables in which words or phrases are defined may be included.

Discuss the table on horses.

Put your finger on the fourth special feature. Tables of important dates are often included in articles.

Discuss the table.

Put your finger on the last special feature. See the second main heading. Next to it is its pronunciation. Who can pronounce the term?

Pronunciations of many unusual and unfamiliar words are given with the article title and also in the text.

Let's see how much information you've mastered about encyclopedias. Turn your ditto over. Take out your pencils and complete the page.

Correct the papers with the students, or collect, correct, and return them later.

FOLLOW-UP

If you have access to some encyclopedias, you may want to do one or both of the following.

1. Assign students to do Worksheet 5.14
2. Assign reports in some subject area requiring encyclopedia research.

Worksheet 5.12 *World Book's* Special Features

World Book's Special Features

On this page and the page that follows, a number of special features of WORLD BOOK are shown. If you make good use of them, even complicated subjects will be easy to understand. Browse through the set and you will find these special features in many articles. Remember, they have been developed to help you get the most out of WORLD BOOK.

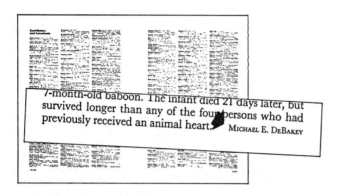

7-month-old baboon. The infant died 21 days later, but survived longer than any of the four persons who had previously received an animal heart. MICHAEL E. DeBAKEY

World Book Contributors sign the articles they write. For information about a contributor, see the list of contributors in Volume A.

Facts in Brief

Capital: Austin.
Government: *Congress*—U.S. senators, 2; U.S. representatives, 27. *Electoral Votes*—29. *State Legislature*—senators, 31; representatives, 150. *Counties*—254.
Area: 266,807 sq. mi. (691,030 km²), including 4,790 sq. mi. (12,407 km²) of inland water but excluding 7 sq. mi. (18 km²) of Gulf of Mexico coastal water; 2nd in

Facts in Brief tables are found in state, province, country, continent, and many other articles. They provide information at a glance.

Horse Terms

Bronco, or **Bronc,** is any untamed western horse.
Colt, technically, is a male horse less than 4 years old. However, the word *colt* is often used for any young horse.
Crossbred means bred from a sire of one breed and a dam of another.
Dam is the mother of a foal.

Tables of Terms present information that defines certain words or phrases used in discussing specialized or highly technical topics.

Important Dates in Connecticut

1614 Adriaen Block claimed Connecticut for the Dutch.
1633 The first English settlement in Connecticut was made in Windsor.
1636 The towns of Hartford, Wethersfield, and Windsor united to form the Connecticut Colony.
1637 Connecticut and other colonies defeated the Pequot Indians in the Pequot War.

Tables of Important Dates are included in many articles. They provide quick reference to outstanding events in the history of a topic.

---

able to use extension methods.

Critically reviewed by the DEPARTMENT OF AGRICULTURE

See also COUNTY AGRICULTURAL EXTENSION AGENT; 4-H.

COUNTY GOVERNMENT. See COUNTY.

COUP D'ÉTAT, *KOO day TAH,* is a sudden take-over of a country's government by a group of conspirators. Usually, the conspirators are public officials who infiltrate and then use their country's armed forces,

Pronunciation of many unusual or unfamiliar words is provided with the article title. Pronunciations are also given for many difficult words that appear in the text. See the **Key to Pronunciation** following this section.

Name _____   Date _____

Worksheet 5.13 Encyclopedias

Write *true* or *false* for each of these:

_____ 1. Some encyclopedias cover all subjects.

_____ 2. Some encyclopedias cover only one subject.

_____ 3. Some encyclopedias are one volume long.

_____ 4. Some encyclopedias are sets of many volumes.

_____ 5. Encyclopedias are usually arranged alphabetically.

_____ 6. Encyclopedias don't have guide words.

_____ 7. Guide words help you alphabetically.

_____ 8. The encyclopedia index can help you find information on a subject that you couldn't have found by looking directly under that subject.

_____ 9. Encyclopedias don't have cross references.

_____ 10. "Related Articles" refers you to other articles pertaining to your subject matter.

If a set of encyclopedias has a volume for each letter of the alphabet, in which volume would you find articles about each of these subjects?

_____ 11. Queen Mary II

_____ 12. Yellowstone National Park

_____ 13. King James I

_____ 14. Babe Ruth

_____ 15. Rainy Lake

Worksheet 5.14 Encyclopedias

1. Identify Daniel Boone in one sentence and give the date of his birth and of his death. _____

_____

_____

_____

2. Football is played mainly in two countries. Name the countries. _____

_____

3. What is California's state motto? _____

_____

_____

4. Identify Zimbabwe in one sentence. _____

_____

5. When was Pierre Auguste Renoir born? _____

6. List three uses of castles. _____

_____

_____

7. Identify Charles Augustus Lindbergh and tell for what he is known. _____

_____

_____

_____

8. Name Canada's two official languages. _____

_____

9. How tall is the Eiffel Tower? _____

10. Where is the Komodo dragon found? _____

_____

Lesson 61. Science Fiction and Nonfiction/Historical Fiction and Nonfiction

OBJECTIVES

1. To teach students to distinguish between science nonfiction and science fiction
2. To teach students to distinguish between historical nonfiction and historical fiction

MATERIALS

Two books to represent each of the following types: science nonfiction, science fiction, historical nonfiction, historical fiction. Separate the books into two stacks, with one type of book in each stack. Some possible selections are

Science nonfiction	Books on lions, tigers, or other easily identifiable subjects
Science fiction	Books with pictures of aliens and so forth on the covers so that immediate identification is possible
Historical nonfiction	A book about Hitler A book about World War I or II
Historical fiction	*Rifles for Watie* *Ox-Cart Man*

PREPARATION

Write this on the board:

> science nonfiction
> science fiction
> historical nonfiction
> historical fiction

LESSON

Who would like to read the names of the four types of books I've listed on the board?

What does nonfiction mean? (true)

What does fiction mean? (not true)

I'm going to show you one book for each of the types on the board, and I'll tell you which type each book is. Afterward I'll show you four books and let you tell me their types.

Hold up *Ox-Cart Man* or another historical fiction book.

> The background of this book is historical—it's true. But the specific story is fiction—not true. This book is historical fiction.

Hold up a science fiction book.

> This book has a science background, but the story is not true. This is science fiction.

Hold up a science nonfiction book.

> This book is about science. It's true. It's nonfiction. It's science nonfiction.

Hold up a book about World War I or II.

> This book is true. It's about a part of history. It's historical nonfiction, a true book about history.

> Now it's your turn. When I hold up a book, raise your hand if you can tell me which type it is.

Hold up a book about Hitler. (If you don't have one, adapt the second paragraph below to fit your substitution.)
Call on someone to identify the book.

> Yes, this is historical nonfiction. Nonfiction means true. Hitler was a real person. He is a part of history. This book is historical nonfiction.

Hold up a science fiction book.
Call on someone to identify it.

> Yes, this is science fiction. Fiction means not true. This book has a science background, but it's not true. It's science fiction.

Hold up a science nonfiction book.
Call on someone to identify it.

> Yes, this book is science nonfiction. Nonfiction means true. The book is about science and it's true. It's science nonfiction.

Hold up *Rifles for Watie* (Wātie).
Call on someone to identify it.

> Watie was not a real person. His story is not true. However, the story takes place during the Civil War and its background is true. So the book is historical fiction—fiction based on history—set in an historical period.

UNIT 6

SIXTH GRADE

What to Teach in Sixth Grade

SUGGESTIONS

1. Before your first trip to the library, refer to Appendix A, "How to Conduct Library Visits."
2. Lessons, reproducible forms, and guidelines for book reports are found in Unit 3. Written book report forms are found in Lesson 35. Oral book report guidelines are in Lesson 36. Use these materials whenever the need arises.
3. You may want to use a green (go) marker and a red (stop) marker to designate the pages you need to teach.

LESSONS

Begin by teaching Lessons 20 ("Book Care and Library Behavior") and 21 ("Appreciating Books") in Unit 3. These lessons need to be retaught each year.

If you know that your students haven't received instruction in library skills, teach Lessons 22A through 61 in Units 3 through 5. Then teach the lessons in this unit. These pages will bring the students up to grade level plus carry them through the lessons for sixth grade.

If you don't know whether your students have had instruction in library skills or if you have reason to believe that they have had instruction, use Pretests 1, 2, and 3 in Appendix B to determine subject mastery. Due to the length of the three tests, you will probably want to give them on three separate days.

If your students do poorly on Pretests 1, 2, and 3, assume either that they have not had library instruction or that they need to have a complete reteaching of previous lessons. For bringing the students up to beginning sixth grade level, teach Lessons 22A through 61 in Units 3 through 5. Thereafter, to cover sixth grade skills, teach the lessons in this unit.

If your students do poorly only on Pretests 2 and 3, bring them up to beginning sixth grade level by teaching Lessons 37 through 61 in Units 4 and 5. Thereafter, to cover sixth grade skills, teach the lessons in this unit.

If your students do poorly only on Pretest 3, bring them up to beginning sixth grade level by teaching Lessons 54 through 61 in Unit 5. Thereafter, to cover sixth grade skills, teach the lessons in this unit.

If your students do well on the pretests except for a couple of items, teach only the lessons related to those specific items to bring the students up to grade level. (The pretest answer page specifies the lesson in which each item is introduced.) After bringing the class up to grade level, teach the lessons in this unit, which cover sixth grade skills.

If your students do well on all of the pretests, they are up to grade level. To cover sixth grade skills, teach the lessons in this unit.

Lesson 62. The Dewey Decimal System

OBJECTIVES

1. To present the Dewey Decimal System of Classification
2. To give the students practice in using the Dewey System

MATERIALS

1. Back-to-back reproductions of Worksheets 6.1 and 6.2
2. Reproductions of Worksheet 6.3

PREPARATION

Copy the following on the board:

_____ Better Basketball
_____ Dinosaurs
_____ Manners for Young People

LESSON

At one time library books were shelved according to when they were purchased. The first book purchased would be first on a shelf. The second book purchased would be second, and so forth.

A librarian named Melvil Dewey thought this was a very inefficient way of arranging books. He thought that nonfiction books should be grouped by subject. If they were, when one was looking for a book about snakes, for example, one would find all the books about snakes in one place. One could examine them and decide which ones to check out. One wouldn't have to run all over the library looking for snake books.

Mr. Dewey not only grouped nonfiction books by subject, he also put all the subjects in a meaningful order.

First, he divided all knowledge into ten main groups. He numbered those groups 000–900 (read: zero hundred through nine hundred).

I'm going to pass a ditto out that shows you how Mr. Dewey arrived at the order within his system.

Distribute back-to-back reproductions of Worksheets 6.1 and 6.2.

Look at these pages as I go over them with you.

The group numbered 000 comes first in the Dewey System, but it's easier to understand if it's discussed last. Therefore, the ditto starts with 100.

To make the order of the subjects meaningful, Melvil Dewey imagined himself to be a prehistoric man, and he asked himself questions he thought such a man would have asked.

The first thing a prehistoric man would want to know would be who he was. He would wonder about himself. Any books dealing with ideas along this line are put in the 100s. The 100s are called Philosophy and Psychology.

Next the prehistoric man would wonder who created him. He thought about God. Religion is 200.

Next the man would look around and notice other people. He would wonder who the man in the next cave was. Books that deal with man's relationships to other people are in the 300s, Social Sciences. Government and Manners are found in the 300s.

The prehistoric man would want to communicate with the man in the next cave. Language is 400. Your ditto says Philology. That was the previous title. We now call the 400s Language. Dictionaries and books in other languages are found in the 400s.

The prehistoric man discovered the world of nature: He discovered animals, plants, the sun, and so forth. Books on these subjects are in Science, 500.

As time passed man learned how to use fire. Perhaps he dropped a clay bowl into the fire and found that after it had been fired, it would hold water. He no longer had to go to the river every time he was thirsty. He could keep a bowl of water in his cave. Man had learned to apply the knowledge he had gained. 600 is Applied Science and Useful Arts. You will find books on cooking and cars in the 600s.

Now man had more time for recreation. He liked to sing, dance, and play games. 700 is called Fine Arts and Recreation. Art, music, dance, photography, and sports are found in the 700s.

Man told stories to his children. Later he wanted to record the stories so other people could have them, too. 800 is Literature. Poems and plays are found in this section.

Man wanted to leave a record of great men he'd known (biography) and of lakes and mountains he'd discovered (geography). He wanted to leave a record of what had happened over the years (history). The 900s cover biography, geography, and history. Usually the 900s are called History.

The 000s actually come first. They come before 100. They have been left until last because they are easier to explain after you've heard about the other numbers. The 000s cover all subjects. They are called General Works. Encyclopedias are in the 000s.

After dividing all knowledge into ten groups and giving each group a hundred numbers, Mr. Dewey discovered that a hundred numbers weren't enough for some groups. He solved the problem by adding a decimal point at the end of the first three numbers and then adding numbers to the other side of the decimal.

Librarians don't write a book's subject on the back of a book. Instead of writing the word *snakes* on the back of a snake book, a code number is written. For snakes the number is 598.1 (read: five ninety-eight point one). When you find the 598.1s, you'll find all of the snake books. Birds are numbered 598.2. Cars are 629.2.

Most libraries use the Dewey Decimal System of Classification.

I'm going to pass out a ditto. At the top you will see a list of the ten main classifications of the Dewey Decimal System.

Distribute Worksheet 6.3.

I have put three book titles on the board. Look at the ditto to find out what number each would have.

We are not dealing with the specific numbers of books right now. We are just concerned with what hundred each is in.

What number would *Better Basketball* have? (700)

What number would *Dinosaurs* have? (500)

Manners for Young People? (300)

Under the ten main classifications on the ditto, you see a list of ten practice items. Do these items by referring to the top half of the page.

Correct the papers with the students, or collect, correct, and return them later.

A STORY ABOUT THE DEWEY DECIMAL SYSTEM OF CLASSIFICATION

(The Story of the Numbers Used for Nonfiction Books)

Some years ago Mr. Melvil Dewey devised a system of classifying books which is used in many libraries. He chose certain main subjects and numbers, so that all nonfiction books on the same subject would be together on the shelf. He chose these subjects by imagining himself to be a prehistoric or primitive man. He asked himself questions he thought such a man would have asked.

100
Who am I?
PHILOSOPHY AND PSYCHOLOGY
(Man thinks about himself.)

200
Who made me?
RELIGION
(Man thinks about God.)

300
Who is the man in the next cave?
SOCIAL SCIENCES
(Man thinks about other people.)

400
How can I make that man understand me?
PHILOLOGY
(Man learns to communicate with others through words.)

500
How can I understand nature and the world about me?
SCIENCE
(Man learns to understand nature on the land, in the sea, and in the sky.)

Reproduced with permission from *School Library Journal,* February 1961.
Copyright R. R. Bowker Company/Cahners Magazine Division.

Worksheet 6.2 The Dewey Decimal System

600

How can I use what I know about nature?

APPLIED SCIENCE AND USEFUL ARTS
(Primitive man learned about fire and how to make weapons. Man through the ages learned about the wheel, about medicine, planting crops, cooking food, building bridges, and how to make all the things we use.)

700

How can I enjoy my leisure time?

FINE ARTS AND RECREATION
(By this time, primitive man had more time to do the things he enjoyed. He learned how to paint pictures and to create music. He also learned how to dance and to play games.)

800

How can I give to my children a record of man's heroic deeds?

LITERATURE
(Man became a storyteller. He created sagas, fables, epics, poetry, and plays about his ancestors and the people he knew. Later, man put these into writing for all people to read.)

900

How can I leave a record for men of the future?

HISTORY   GEOGRAPHY   BIOGRAPHY
(So man began to write about events that had occurred everywhere, and about people who had participated in these events.)

000

GENERAL WORKS
The numbers up to 100 are used for bibliographies, books about books, and for books which contain information on many subjects such as encyclopedias and other reference books.

Worksheet 6.3 The Dewey Decimal System of Classification

NUMBERS	GROUP NAME	SUBJECTS COVERED
000–099	General Works	Encyclopedias
100–199	Philosophy	What people think
200–299	Religion	Religion, mythology
300–399	Social Sciences	Government, careers, manners, folklore
400–499	Language	Dictionaries, books in other languages
500–599	Pure Science	Mathematics, astronomy, nature (animals, plants, rocks, etc.)
600–699	Applied Science	Airplanes, cars, homemaking
700–799	Fine Arts and Recreation	Art, photography, music, sports
800–899	Literature	Poetry, plays, other literature
900–999	History	History, geography, biography, travel

Write the general Dewey classification number for each title.

Example: <u>900</u> <u>History of the World</u>

_____ 1. <u>Football Basics</u>

_____ 2. <u>Poems of Earth and Space</u>

_____ 3. <u>California Government</u>

_____ 4. <u>Whales and Dolphins</u>

_____ 5. <u>The United States in World War I</u>

_____ 6. <u>Webster's Dictionary</u>

_____ 7. <u>The Bible</u>

_____ 8. <u>The World Book Encyclopedia</u>

_____ 9. <u>Cars and Trucks</u>

_____ 10. <u>An Introduction to Philosophy</u>

Lesson 63. Card Catalog Review and Historical Periods

OBJECTIVES

1. To review catalog cards
2. To review how to differentiate between an author, title, and subject card
3. To teach the students how historical periods are filed in the card catalog

MATERIALS

1. A chalkboard, chalk, and eraser
2. Reproductions of Worksheet 6.4

PREPARATIONS

1. Copy this catalog card on the chalkboard. Be sure to capitalize the first line.

```
                    INSECTS

    595.7    Gannon, Robert
    Gan            What's under a rock?    Illus.
             by Stefan Martin.    Dutton 1971
                  122p.    Illus.
```

2. Copy these two lines on the chalkboard. Be sure to capitalize them.

U.S. HISTORY.   REVOLUTION
U.S. HISTORY.   CIVIL WAR

LESSON

Let's look at the catalog card on the board.

What's the title of the book? (*What's Under a Rock?*)

Who is the author? (Robert Gannon)

How many pages are in the book? (122 pages)

Who is the publisher? (Dutton)

Who is the illustrator? (Stefan Martin)

What is the class number? (595.7)

What is the call number? (595.7 Gan)

What does "Gan" stand for? (Gannon)

Is the book fiction or nonfiction? (nonfiction)

How do you know? (Nonfiction books have numbers.)

What is the copyright date? (1971)

What does "illus." on the last line mean? (There are pictures in the book.)

What kind of card is it? (subject)

How do you know? (The first line is in capitals.)

Erase INSECTS.

What kind of card is this now? (author)

How do you know? (The author's name is on the first line.)

Write the title where INSECTS was.

What kind of card is this now? (a title card)

How do you know? (The title is on the first line.)

Generally speaking, there are three cards in the card catalog for each book. What are they? (author, subject, and title cards)

Which three words are disregarded if they are first words in a title? (a, an, the)

How is the card catalog arranged? (alphabetically)

Yes, generally speaking, it is. There are some exceptions to that rule. Historical periods are located alphabetically under the name of the country and the subject to which they relate. In other words, if you were looking up an historical period relating to the United States, you would look under U.S. HISTORY—U.S. for the country and history for the subject. Second, you would locate the specific historical period chronologically.

What does *chronologically* mean? (according to time, according to when an event happened)

If you want a book about the Civil War, you must look under the country first. You can't just look under civil war. Do you mean the Russian civil war, the Chinese civil war? You probably mean the U.S. Civil War. If you want a book about the U.S. Civil War, look under the country and the subject—U.S. HISTORY. Then look chronologically until you find the historical period—CIVIL WAR.

Look at the board.

Point to:

      U.S. HISTORY.   REVOLUTION
      U.S. HISTORY.   CIVIL WAR

First you find the country and subject—U.S. HISTORY—alphabetically. Then you look chronologically for the historical period—CIVIL WAR.

Does Revolution come alphabetically before Civil War? (no)

The Revolution came before the Civil War in time—chronologically.

Historical periods are located first under the countries to which they relate and the subject history. Second, they are located chronologically— by time. Sometimes librarians say loosely that history is arranged chronologically, but they mean that it is arranged chronologically under the country and the subject, which are arranged alphabetically.

Some libraries have a card at the beginning of historical periods which lists all of the periods chronologically. If there is such a card, it will be of help to you.

I'm going to distribute a ditto for you to do. It will reveal how well you understand what I've taught you today.

Distribute the ditto.
Correct the dittos with the students, or collect, correct, and return them later.

Name _____   Date _____

Worksheet 6.4 The Card Catalog

Write the letters of the answers below to the matching items.

1. _____

2. _____

3. _____

4. _____

5. _____

6. _____

7. _____

8. _____

796.334
Jac

Jackson, Caary Paul
How to play better soccer.
Illustrated by Don Madden. Crowell
1978

151p.   illus.

Answers

a. copyright date   c. illustrations   e. publisher   g. illustrator
b. pages   d. title   f. author   h. call number

9. Generally speaking, there are three cards in the card catalog for each book. Name them.

_____, _____,

_____

10. Which of the above has the first line in capitals? _____

_____

11. List three words that are disregarded when they are used as first words in a title.

_____, _____, _____

12. If CLEMENS, SAMUEL LANGHORNE appeared on the top line of a catalog card, how would you know the book was about him? _____

_____

13. How are historical periods filed in the card catalog? _____

_____

_____

14. Which books are true: fiction or nonfiction? _____

15. What is an illustrator? _____

_____

Lesson 64. Card Catalog Practice

OBJECTIVES

1. To teach students how to use the card catalog to locate a book
2. To give students practice using the card catalog via a ditto

MATERIAL

Back-to-back reproductions of Worksheets 6.5 and 6.6

LESSON

Do you have to know a book's author to be able to find a book in the library? (no)

What else could you know that would lead you to the book you want? (the title or the subject)

So really you only have to know one of three things: the author or the title or the subject.

I'm going to distribute a ditto. Don't take out your pencils.

Pass out reproductions of Worksheets 6.5 and 6.6.

Look at Worksheet 6.5. We are going to discuss this page. You are not to write on it.

At the top of the page you see a card catalog. Underneath you see these words: Do you know the author, title, or subject for the books below? In which drawer would each be found?

Remember, in alphabetizing titles, there are three words we disregard if they are first words of titles. What are they? (a, an, the)

Look at item 1. A book about motorcycles.

Do you know the author of the book? (no)

Do you know the title? (no)

Do you know the subject? (yes, motorcycles)

If we were writing on the page, you'd put "subject" in the first column.

In which drawer would you find motorcycles? (L–M)

If we were writing on the page, you'd put "L–M" in the second column.

What do you know about item 2? (the book title)

In which drawer would you look? (R)

What do you know about item 3? (the author)

In which drawer would you look? (E–F)

What do you know about item 4? (the title)

In which drawer would you look? (V–Z)

What do you know about item 5? (the subject)

In which drawer would you look? (L–M)

What do you know about item 6? (the title)

In which drawer would you look? (T–U)

What do you know about item 7? (the subject)

In which drawer would you look? (L–M)

What do you know about item 8? (the author)

In which drawer would you look? (E–F)

What do you know about item 9? (the author)

In which drawer would you look? (G)

What do you know about item 10? (the title)

In which drawer would you look? (T–U)

We've done ten practice items together. Let's see what you can do by yourself. Turn your paper over. Take out your pencils and complete Worksheet 6.6. Don't do Worksheet 6.5. We did that together.

SUGGESTION

On another day, you may want to assign Worksheet 6.5 as a review.

Name _____   Date _____

Worksheet 6.5 The Card Catalog

A	D	H	N	S
B	E-F	I-K	O-Q	T-U
C	G	L-M	R	V-Z

Do you know the author, title, or subject for the books below? In which drawer would each be found?

	Author Title Subject	Drawer
1. A book about motorcycles	_____	_____
2. The book Rabbit Hill	_____	_____
3. A book by Walter Farley	_____	_____
4. The book The Wizard of Oz	_____	_____
5. A book about Mexico	_____	_____
6. The book Trapped	_____	_____
7. A book about lions	_____	_____
8. A book by Don Freeman	_____	_____
9. A book by Paul Galdone	_____	_____
10. The book A Trip to Hawaii	_____	_____

Worksheet 6.6 The Card Catalog

A	D	H	N	S
B	E-F	I-K	O-Q	T-U
C	G	L-M	R	V-Z

Do you know the author, title, or subject for the books below? In which drawer would each be found?

	Author Title Subject	**Drawer**
1. A book by Marcia Brown	_____	____
2. The book An Eagle Returns	_____	____
3. A book about monsters	_____	____
4. The book You Never Can Tell	_____	____
5. A book about cats	_____	____
6. A book by Bill Peet	_____	____
7. The book The Last Unicorn	_____	____
8. A book by Beverly Cleary	_____	____
9. The book A Present for Mary	_____	____
10. A book about jokes	_____	____

Lesson 65. Catalog Card Arrangement

OBJECTIVES

1. To teach students how catalog cards are arranged
2. To test comprehension with a follow-up ditto

MATERIALS

1. A chalkboard, chalk, and eraser
2. Reproductions of Worksheet 6.7

PREPARATION

Copy the following on the board. Don't include the answers in parentheses.

Set 1:

_____	How to Cook	(4)
_____	An Evening in Rome	(2)
_____	Andy's Wish	(1)
_____	A Fresh Start	(3)

Set 2:

_____	Seascapes	(7)
_____	St. George	(6)
_____	Dogs	(2)
_____	Dr. Dolittle	(1)
_____	Mr. Revere and I	(3)
_____	Mittens for Joe	(4)
_____	101 Dalmatians	(5)

Set 3:

_____	North America	(2)
_____	United States	(3)
_____	Air pollution	(1)

LESSON

We've been studying about the card catalog.

Who remembers the order in which catalog cards are arranged? (alphabetical)

There are three words that are disregarded if they are the first words of a title. What are they? (a, an, the)

For visual impact, write on the board: a, an, the.

I've put some filing practice items on the board. Some items are underlined. What does the underlining signify (mean)? (They are book titles.)

Who would like to come number the first set in order?

Point to the first set of practice items.
Suggest that the student cross off any words he or she is not going to use. (a, an, the)
After a student has numbered the items in correct order, discuss what has been done and why.

When looking in the card catalog one needs to know that abbreviated words are filed as if they were spelled out.

Write these on the board:

> St.
> Dr.
> Mr.

As you get the answer to each of the next three questions, write the full spelling next to the abbreviations you have already put on the board.

How do you spell St.? (Saint)

Dr.? (Doctor)

Mr.? (Mister)

You must think of abbreviated words as if they were spelled out when you look for them in the card catalog. An exception is Mrs. It is filed exactly as it appears.

We've spelled abbreviations out here on the board for demonstration, but in general practice one just spells the words out mentally.

Numbers are filed as if they were spelled out.

Write on the board: 100 Story Poems
Under 100, write: One hundred

Mentally spell out one hundred.

Write this on the board: McDonald.

Names beginning with Mc are filed as if they were spelled Mac.

On the board cross out Mc and write: Mac.

> Who would like to number the second set in order?

Discuss what the student did and why.

> If you are looking for a subject that has two words, look under the first word.

Write on the board: New England.

> Look under the first word: New.

> Who would like to number the last set in order?

Discuss what the student did and why.

> When using the card catalog, go by the rules you have just been taught.

> Libraries that are putting their card catalog information into computers may go by new rules. According to the rules for computers (*ALA Filing Rules,* American Library Association, 1980), one is to look under an entry exactly as it appears. That means abbreviations are not spelled out. It will probably be quite some time before most libraries change from a card catalog format to computers. In the meantime, always start with the rules you were taught at the beginning of this lesson: mentally spell abbreviations out.

> I am going to pass out a ditto of practice items. Take your pencils out of your desks and get ready to do the paper.

Distribute the ditto.

It's very effective to correct and discuss the papers individually as each student finishes.

Worksheet 6.7 The Card Catalog: Catalog Card Arrangement

1. Catalog cards are arranged alphabetically by their first words. (Disregard the words *a, an,* and *the* when they are the first words in a title.) Number these titles in order.

   _____ At Home in India

   _____ An Eagle's Journey

   _____ Loner

   _____ The Midnight Express

   _____ Seventeen

2. Abbreviations and numbers are filed as if they were spelled out. Number these titles in order.

   _____ Mr. Revere and I

   _____ 100 Poems About People

   _____ Dr. Elizabeth

   _____ St. Patrick

   _____ Dogs of America

   _____ Mother's Day

   _____ Some Friend!

3. Names that begin with Mc are filed as if they were spelled Mac. Number these names in order.

   _____ McCormick

   _____ MacDaniel

   _____ McCowan

   _____ McCall

   _____ MacGraw

4. If a subject is made up of two or more words, it is filed by the first word. Number these subjects in order.

   _____ South Sea Islands

   _____ Soccer—Rules

   _____ Television Broadcasting

Lesson 66. Card Catalog Review and Tracing

OBJECTIVES

1. To review catalog cards
2. To explain (or review) what a tracing is
3. To give students practice identifying author, subject, and title cards

MATERIALS

1. Reproductions of Worksheets 6.8 and 6.9 (Schools without libraries: Don't put these pages back to back.)
2. Schools with libraries: A card catalog

PREPARATION

Schools with libraries: Schedule a library visit.

Schools without libraries: Adapt this lesson for your use. Let students use Worksheet 6.8 instead of the card catalog to do the assignment on Worksheet 6.9.

LESSON

Today we're going to review catalog cards. Then we're going to the library where half of you will locate author, subject, and title cards in the card catalog. The other half will browse and check out books. At our next visit to the library, the groups will rotate.

I'm going to pass out reproductions of some sample cards.

Distribute reproductions of Worksheets 6.8 and 6.9.

Look at Worksheet 6.8. The three cards pictured here are for three different books.

Which of the cards is the title card? (the last one)

How do you know? (The title is on the first line. In this case, the title is on the first two lines.)

Which of the cards is the subject card? (the second)

How do you know? (The first line is capitalized.)

Which of the cards is the author card? (the first)

How do you know? (The author is on the first line.)

Look at the first card.

Who is the author of this book? (Jean Craighead George)

What is the title? (*My Side of the Mountain*)

How many pages are in the book? (178 pages)

Are there any pictures? (yes)

How do you know? (The third line says, "illustrated by Jean George." The fifth line says, "illus.," which means illustrations—pictures.)

Who is the publisher? (Dutton)

What is the call number? (Geo)

When was the book copyrighted? (1959)

If your students need more practice with this type of identification, repeat the questions above for the remaining two cards. If not, go on.

There is some information at the bottom of the cards. Does anyone know what it's for and what it's called? (The information at the bottom of the cards is for the librarian. It tells the librarian which cards are filed for each book. It's called a *tracing*.)

Turn your paper over to Worksheet 6.9, the assignment page.

Notice that you are to find an author card, a title card, and a subject card.

You will get all of your information out of one drawer of the card catalog; therefore, the three cards will be for different books.

Just start looking through your drawer of cards until you find an author's name on the top line. That will be an author card. Fill in the information on the ditto for the author card.

Look through the drawer until you find a card that has a title on the first line. That will be a title card. Fill in the information on the paper for the title card.

Look through the drawer until you find a card that has the first line in capitals. That will be a subject card. Fill in the information on the paper for the subject card.

Remember, you are to get all of your information from one drawer; therefore, the information will be for three different books.

Today the girls (or boys) will do the assignment. Be sure to take your papers to the library.

Will the students who won't be doing the assignment today, please pass their papers in.

If the students need to take pencils with them, remind them now.

At the Library

1. Have the class enter the library in two groups: those who will be doing the assignment and those who will be checking books out.

2. Everyone should be seated with his or her own group.

3. Excuse a few of the students who are doing the assignment to get card catalog drawers. Have them take the drawers to their tables. Continue until all of the students in the assignment group have card catalog drawers.

4. Excuse the group that will be browsing and checking books out.

5. Circulate among those doing the assignment. Pause and compare a few lines from a student's paper against the catalog card he or she is copying. Grade that part of the paper on the spot. Continue.

   Checking papers without the catalog will be fairly easy. The first line of each card should start with the same letter. If a student has the "S" drawer, the author's last name, the subject, and the title will all start with "S," if the student has done the paper as assigned.

   When students hand you their finished papers, if possible, grade and discuss their work with them right then.

6. Students who finish their assignments early should give their papers to you and then check out books.

FOLLOW-UP

Before going to the library next week, review one or more catalog cards. (Worksheet 4.23 has three catalog cards you may want to reproduce for this review.) Also review how to do the assignment. (See the second half of this lesson.)

Take your class to the library and rotate the groups.

Geo   George, Jean Craighead
       My side of the mountain, written
and illustrated by Jean George.
Dutton   1959
      178p.   illus.

   I.   Title

BASEBALL CARDS

769.5   Clark, Steve
Cla   The complete book of baseball
cards. Grosset and Dunlap   1976
      112p.   illus.

   1.   Baseball cards   I.   T

Betty Crocker's Cookbook for boys
and girls

641.5   Crocker, Betty
Cro   Betty Crocker's Cookbook for boys
and girls.   Golden Press   1984
      94p.   illus.

   1.   Cookery   I.   T

Worksheet 6.9 Card Catalog Practice

Author Card

> Author _____
>
> Title _____
>
> Illustrator _____
>
> Publisher _____
>
> Copyright Date _____ Number of Pages _____
>
> Call Number _____

Title Card

> Title _____
>
> Author _____
>
> Illustrator _____
>
> Publisher _____
>
> Copyright Date _____ Number of Pages _____
>
> Call Number _____

Subject Card

> Subject _____
>
> Author _____
>
> Title _____
>
> Illustrator _____
>
> Publisher _____
>
> Copyright Date _____ Number of Pages _____
>
> Call Number _____

Lesson 67. Biography and Autobiography

OBJECTIVES

1. To teach the meaning and call numbers of biography, collective biography, and autobiography
2. To provide some follow-up activities

MATERIALS

1. A biography (Libraries shelve biographies under 921, 92, or B.)
2. A chalkboard, chalk, and eraser
3. Reproductions of Worksheet 6.10

PREPARATION

If you have a school library, find out how biographies are shelved so you can use that information in teaching this lesson. If you don't have a library, teach this lesson as it is.

LESSON

Hold up a biography.

> This a biography about _____ . A biography is the story of a person's life, written by another person.
>
> This book is the true story of _____ 's life. It was written by _____ . This is a biography.

Biographies are shelved one of several ways. Some libraries shelve them under 921. Others shelve them under 92. And some libraries shelve them under B, which stands for *biography*.

If you have a school library, tell your students how it shelves biographies. Write on the board:

> 614   921
> Smi   Was

The letters under a class number are always taken from the beginning of the author's last name, except for individual biography and autobiography.

The "Smi" under 614 stands for the beginning of the author's last name.

The letters under 921 (92 or B) are *not* the author's letters. They are letters from the biographee's last name. The *biographee* is the person the book is about.

Point to "921 Was" on the board.

This call number says the book is a biography. 921 means biography. "Was" means the book is about a person whose last name starts with these three letters.

If you want a biography about Abraham Lincoln, you can go right to one without using the card catalog. Look under 921 Lin.

What call number would you look under to find a book about Christopher Columbus? (921 Col)

Clara Barton? (921 Bar)

George Washington? (921 Was)

There are some books that contain several biographies. These books are called *collective biographies*.

You know what a collection is—something you gather together. You may have a collection of baseball cards or photographs or stamps.

A collective biography is a book that has a number of biographies in it. A collective biography is shelved under 920.

Write on the board:

> 920
> Mil

The letters under 920 can't be the beginning of the biographee's last name, can they? There isn't just one biographee. Therefore, the letters are the author's letters.

The number 920 means collective biography. "Mil" is the beginning of the author's last name.

The Story of My Life by Helen Keller is an autobiography. "Auto" means self.

An autobiography is a self biography—the story of one's life, written by oneself.

Helen Keller wrote the true story of her own life in *The Story of My Life*. She wrote an autobiography.

Autobiographies are shelved among the biographies. Helen Keller's autobiography would have this call number.

Write on the board:

921
Kel

The "Kel" stands for Keller—the person the book is about.

Let's see how much you remember.

Ask these questions.

1. What is a biography? (the true story of a person's life, written by another person)
2. What is the class number for individual biography—a biography about one person? (921 or 92. Some libraries shelve biographies under "B.")
3. What do the letters under 921 stand for? (the last name of the person the book is about)
4. Under what number would you find a biography of Kit Carson? (921 Car)
5. What is a collective biography? (a collection of biographies)
6. What is the class number for collective biography? (920)
7. What do the letters under 920 stand for? (the author's last name)
8. What is the call number for a book by John Smith entitled *Famous Writers?* (920 Smi)
9. What is an autobiography? (the story of one's life, written by oneself)
10. Where are autobiographies shelved? (in the 921s)
11. What do the letters under 921 stand for? (the name of the person the book is about)
12. What is the call number for an autobiography by Ben Franklin? (921 Fra)

Inform the students that you are going to distribute a ditto for them to study and complete.

Pass out reproductions of Worksheet 6.10.

FOLLOW-UP

Select from the following suggestions:

1. Ask your students to write autobiographies.
2. Ask your students to write biographies about their classmates.

3. If you have a library, ask your students to read a biography or autobiography. (There are usually very few autobiographies, so be sure to tell the students they may read *either* a biography or an autobiography.)

4. If you have a library that has biographical reference books about authors, introduce the books to your students. Then ask your students to write a report about one of their favorite authors. See Worksheet 6.11 for an author report form.

Name _____   Date _____

Worksheet 6.10 Biography and Autobiography

Study these definitions.

A *biography* is a true story of a person's life, written by another person.

A *collective biography* is a collection of biographies.

An *autobiography* is a self biography—a true story of one's life, written by oneself.

Study how biography and autobiography are shelved.

Individual biography and *autobiography* are shelved under 921. (Some libraries shelve them under 92 or B.) The letters under 921 (92 or B) represent *the name of the person the book is about*. The only number in the Dewey Decimal System that is not followed by the letters of the author's name is 921 (92 or B).

Collective biography is shelved under 920. The letters under the number represent *the author's name*.

Write the call numbers for these books.

	Title	**Author**
1. _____	Famous Spies	Frank Surge
2. _____	Abe Lincoln, the Young Years	Keith Brandt
3. _____	Indian Chiefs	Lynne Deur
4. _____	Harry Houdini, Master of Magic	Robert Kraske
5. _____	Famous Chess Players	Peter M. Lerner
6. _____	Nellie Bly	Iris Noble
7. _____	The First Book of Presidents	Harold Coy
8. _____	Kit Carson and the Wild Frontier	Ralph Moody
9. _____	Five Artists of the Old West	Clide Hollmann
10. _____	Heroes of the American Revolution	Burke Davis

Worksheet 6.11 Author Report

Name of the author _____

Personal (birthplace, birth date, family, education, home) _____

_____

_____

_____

_____

_____

_____

Interests (hobbies, etc.) _____

_____

_____

_____

Career (previous and current occupations, awards) _____

_____

_____

_____

Writings (what the author has written) _____

_____

_____

_____

_____

Sidelights (other information you came across) _____

_____

_____

_____

_____

PART 2

Appendices

APPENDIX A
HOW TO CONDUCT LIBRARY VISITS

Preliminary Considerations

If you don't have a librarian or a schoolwide standard for library visits, you may want to consider the following visitation plan. Note that this plan is quite formal. Students at the elementary school level require a formal approach. It gives them security and provides them with a structure of discipline that can easily be maintained by the teacher.

Before taking your class to the library, visit and find out which books your students are supposed to use. Also find out if there are any rules of which you should be aware.

Teachers of second through sixth grades may want their students to use markers to help them replace books correctly on the shelves. If the library doesn't supply markers, make your own. Cut chipboard or preferably something stiffer into strips measuring 10 by 3 inches. Make a marker for each of your students, plus a few extra ones. Put them in an open box. The use of markers is explained in detail later in this appendix.

There are three ways pencils can be supplied in the library.

1. The library can provide a box of pencils for each library table that your class will use.
2. Each student can take his or her own pencil to the library.
3. You can take and bring back one to four pencil boxes for your students' use.

In the Classroom

Discuss the fact that the library is a place of quiet.

If you need to take pencil boxes to the library, assign a pencil monitor to take care of this task. If each student is going to take his or her own pencil to the library, remind the class of this.

If you don't have a door monitor, assign one.

Grades two through six may each need to assign a monitor to take markers to the library. If you don't plan to use markers, or if the library will provide them, you won't need to be concerned.

258

At the Library

1. Pause outside the library, and reiterate that the library is a place of quiet.
2. Have your door monitor hold the library door open.
3. Tell the students to enter the library quietly.
4. The first student should walk to the last table to be used by your class. If the tables are rectangular, he or she should take the last seat. The students thereafter should follow. There is no decision making on the part of the students as to where each will sit. The pattern is always that the first student takes the last seat, and each student thereafter fills up the next seat until everyone is seated.
5. If there is only one class scheduled for the library at a time, you will want to teach some lessons in the library. For example, the first time your students go to the library, you should teach them how to replace books on a shelf. Not only does this lesson need to be taught every year to kindergarten through sixth grade, it should be taught throughout the year as needed.

How to Replace Books on a Shelf

Sometimes when people go to the library, they don't replace books on the shelves properly.

Today let's learn the correct way to put a book back on a shelf. First of all, when we put a book back on the shelf, we put it right side up with the spine facing out.

The spine is the part of the book you see when the book is shelved.

Point to the spine of a book: the 1 to 3 inch strip that joins the front and back covers. (See the glossary for a picture.)

The name of the book is on the spine. This book is _____.

If the books were turned with the open edges facing out, we wouldn't know which books they were.

Demonstrate.

Sometimes when we put a book on the shelf, we catch another book inside our book. This can cause pages to be damaged.

Demonstrate how one book can be caught inside another.

Use your free hand to make an opening for the book before you reshelve it.

Who would like to show us how to put a book back on the shelf?

Call on several students, one at a time, to demonstrate.

We don't put a book on top of a row of books or on the outside of a bookend. We put the book back in its right place. If we don't know where a book goes, we lay it on the table.

Other Things to Teach

Tell the students that if they check a book out, they must keep that book and take it to the classroom. They can't reshelve it. This needs to be stressed with all classes, especially kindergarten.

Show the students where to place the books that they will be returning on their next visit. (This could be taught as you enter the library on your second visit, unless you think there is a need for it now.)

On your first visit, teach any rules native to your own library.

After the library lesson, prepare the students to get books.

Getting Books

Kindergarten and First Grade

Show your students the books from which they may select. Kindergarten and first grade classes will probably be limited to picture books.

If the picture books are not in order, the students can put books they don't want any place in the picture book section. If this is not the case, confer with the person in charge of the library as to how to handle replacement of picture books.

Tell the students that after you excuse them to get a book, they may go to the shelves.

When they find a book that they want to borrow (check out), they are to take the book to the main desk.

Say that you will be at the main desk to print their names and room number on the book cards so that you or the clerk can check the books out to them.

After checking out books, the students are to sit down and read until it's time to go.

Excuse one table of students to go to the shelves. The other students are to remain seated. After a few students have found their books, excuse another table to go to the shelves. Continue until all of the students have books.

If you have an aide, one of you should watch the students replace books on the shelves. The students will need help reshelving books throughout the year.

If a librarian or library clerk will be writing students' names and checking books out, you can maintain order and help students replace books correctly.

At the end of the period, tell the students to close their books and get ready to go back to the room.

Comment on whether the students have left the shelves in good condition or not. If there is a book on top of a row of books, on the wrong side of the bookends, or with the page edges facing out, call on someone to make the necessary correction while the class watches.

Have your door monitor take his or her position.

Excuse a table of students at a time to line up at the door. Check to see if the students are carrying their books properly. Books should be carried under the arm or against the chest.

Proceed back to your room.

Second Through Sixth Grades

Teachers of second grade students should write their students' names on book cards for them until after Lesson 19 in Unit 2, "How to Fill Out a Book Card," has been taught.

Students in grades 3 through 6 should be able to fill out their own book cards. However, you may need to remind them, at the beginning of the year, to write their first and last names and their room number.

Tell your students from which books they may select. At these grade levels the policy may be to allow classes free use of the entire library. Check to make sure.

If you are going to have the students use markers, explain how they are to be used. Say that each student is to use a marker when he or she removes a book from a shelf. The student should slip the marker in between the book he or she plans to remove and its neighbor. If a student doesn't want the book that was removed from the shelf, the marker will show where to replace it. If the student decides to check the book out, he or she should remove the marker and put it in the marker box.

Tell your students that when you excuse them, they are to get their books, check them out, and sit down and read until it's time to go.

Excuse the students, a table at a time, at fifteen-second intervals.

Allowing all second graders to go to the shelves at the same time may not be appropriate. If the students are not self-disciplined, excuse only one or two tables at a time to go to the shelves. After some of the students at the shelves find their books, excuse the last tables.

Maintain order during the period.

Before leaving the library, comment on whether the students have left the shelves in good condition or not. If there is a book on top of a row, on the wrong side of the bookends, or with the page edges facing out, call on someone to make the necessary correction while the class watches.

At the end of the period, excuse the door monitor to take his or her post.

Excuse students to line up, a table at a time. Check to see if the students are carrying their books properly. Books should be carried under the arm or against the chest.

Proceed back to the room.

APPENDIX B
PRETESTS AND ANSWERS

Fourth, fifth, and sixth grade teachers may want to pretest their students. Considerations relative to pretesting are covered in detail at the beginning of the fourth, fifth, and sixth grade units under the title What to Teach in _____ Grade. Specific references as to which pretest to use are repeated below. For full explanatory information, see the beginning of the appropriate unit.

Fourth Grade, Pretest 1

If you don't know whether your students have had instruction in library skills or if you have reason to believe that they have had instruction, use Pretest 1 to determine subject mastery.

Fifth Grade, Pretests 1 and 2

If you don't know whether your students have had instruction in library skills or if you have reason to believe that they have had instruction, use Pretests 1 and 2 to determine subject mastery. You may want to give Pretest 1 on one day and Pretest 2 on another day. If you want to give both tests on the same day, reproduce the pretests as double-sided dittos.

Sixth Grade, Pretests 1, 2, and 3

If you don't know whether your students have had instruction in library skills or if you have reason to believe that they have had instruction, use Pretests 1, 2, and 3 to determine subject mastery. Due to the length of the three tests, you will probably want to give them on three separate days.

Pretest 1

PAGE 1

Look in the first box below. Write the letter for each answer.

1. _____ the name of a book

2. _____ a person who writes a book

3. _____ a person who creates the pictures for a book

4. _____ a company that makes a book and sells it

5. _____ where a book is made

6. _____ proof that one owns the rights to a book

```
a.  publisher
b.  illustrator
c.  title
d.  place of publication
e.  copyright
f.  author
```

Complete each sentence using the terms from the box below.

7. The title, author, illustrator, publisher, and place of publication are found on _____

_____.

8. A little dictionary in the back of a book is called _____.

9. A list of the chapters or stories in a book is called _____.

10. A list of subjects in a book and the pages where they are found is called _____

_____.

```
a table of contents
an index
a title page
a glossary
```

Pretest 1

A Light in the Dark

by Nan Green

illustrated by Don Burns

Blue River Press
New York

Read the title page above, then write the following:

1. Publisher _____

2. Author _____

3. Title _____

4. Illustrator _____

5. Place of publication _____

Pretest 2

PAGE 1

Fill in the blank spaces using the answers in the box below.

1. Books that are not true are called _____.

2. Fiction books are shelved by _____.

3. Fiction books that are easy to read are called _____.

4. Short stories are shelved in fiction or in the _____ section of the library.

5. Three words disregarded as first words of titles are _____.

6. Books that are true are called _____.

7. Nonfiction is arranged on the shelves by _____.

8. Books that can't be checked out and are not meant to be read all the way through are called _____ books.

9. The _____ tells you where to find books in a library.

10. _____ give you alphabetical help in finding the card you want in a drawer of catalog cards.

```
numbers
guide cards
fiction
easy books
story collection
card catalog
reference
nonfiction
author's last name
of, in, it
a, an, the
```

Pretest 2

PAGE 2

Copy these fiction books in order below.

Blue Willow	Ginger Pye	Drag Strip	The Wind Blows Free	The Hundred Dresses
Gates	Estes	Gault	Erdman	Estes
Gat	Est	Gau	Erd	Est

Name _____   Date _____

Pretest 2

PAGE 3

Copy these nonfiction books in order below.

Books	Ponies	Insect Pets	Goats	Rabbits
Bartlett	Robison	Stevens	Bronson	Silverstein
655 Bar	636.16 Rob	638 Ste	636.3 Bro	636.9 Sil

Pretest 2

PAGE 4

```
629.2        Burton, Bill
Bur              Cars, cars, cars; illus. by
             Joe Howard.    Sweetwater Press
             1984
                  206p.    illus.
```

Identify the following. Write your answers on the lines.

1. Illustrator   _____

2. Call number   _____

3. Publisher   _____

4. Author   _____

5. Number of pages   _____

6. Title   _____

7. Copyright date   _____

GUIDE CARDS
Kenya/king
king/Kipling
Kipling/kites
kites/knight

Between which of the guide cards above would you find these?

8. Klondike   _____

9. Jean Brown Kinney   _____

10. Kit Carson, Mountain Man   _____

Pretest 3

PAGE 1

Fill in the blank spaces using the answers in the box below.

1. One needs to be concerned about the copyright date when selecting _____

   _____ books.

2. _____ means pen name: a name assumed by an author, which is not his or her own.

3. A catalog card that has the illustrator's name on the top line is called _____

   _____ .

4. A brief description of a book's story or contents on a catalog card is called _____

   _____ .

5. A catalog card that refers to a subject which is just a part of a book is called a _____

   _____ .

6. Dictionaries deal with words. Encyclopedias deal with _____

   _____ .

7. If you can't find the information you need by looking directly for it in an encyclopedia, you

   should look in the _____ .

8. What three things might you know about a book that will enable you to find it in the card

   catalog? _____

   _____

9. This is a _____ book. →

598.2	Smith, Joe
Smi	Birds.

10. This is a _____ book. →

Ada	Adams, Alice
	Birds.

nonfiction	subject analytic card
an annotation	articles
an illustrator card	fiction
pseudonym	index
science and geography	author, subject, title

Name _____   **Date** _____

Pretest 3

PAGE 2   Write <u>true</u> or <u>false</u> for the first ten items below.

_____ 1. "See" and "see also" catalog cards are cross references.

_____ 2. A "see also" reference directs you to additional material related to your subject.

_____ 3. A "see" reference directs you to a different heading.

_____ 4. Some encyclopedias are one-volume; other encyclopedias have more than one volume.

_____ 5. Some encyclopedias are about all subjects; others are about only one subject.

_____ 6. Encyclopedias are not reference books.

_____ 7. Reference books are designed to be read from cover to cover.

_____ 8. Encyclopedias are usually arranged alphabetically.

_____ 9. Encyclopedias have guide words.

_____ 10. Encyclopedias don't have cross references.

What type of book is each of these? Find the answers in the box below.

11. <u>Little House on the Prairie</u>   _____

12. <u>Abraham Lincoln</u>   _____

13. <u>Lions</u>   _____

14. <u>Aliens in Space</u>   _____

```
science fiction
historical fiction
science nonfiction
historical nonfiction
```

If an encyclopedia set has one volume for each letter of the alphabet, in which volume would you find each of these:

15. Bridge of Sighs   _____

16. Queen Beatrix   _____

17. Book Week   _____

18. Horse racing   _____

19. Mountain lion   _____

20. King William I   _____

Pretest 3

PAGE 3

Mac   MacLachlan, Patricia
                 Sarah, plain and tall.
          Harper and Row 1985
               58p.

1. Who is the publisher? _____

2. What is the title? _____

3. Who is the author? _____

4. How many pages are in the book? _____

5. What does "Mac" stand for? _____

6. What is the copyright date? _____

7. Is the book fiction or nonfiction? _____

8. How do you know? _____

_____

9. Are there any illustrations? _____

10. What is the call number? _____

Answers to Pretest 1

If the class lacks mastery of specific items, reteach the material. See the pages below, which designate where the items were introduced.

PRETEST 1:   Page 1

Answers	Where Introduced	
	Unit	Lesson
1. c	3	23A/23B
2. f	3	23A/23B
3. b	3	24
4. a	3	25
5. d	3	25
6. e	3	25
7. a title page	3	25
8. a glossary	3	32
9. a table of contents	3	30
10. an index	3	33

PRETEST 1:   Page 2

Answers	Where Introduced	
	Unit	Lesson
1. Blue River Press	3	25
2. Nan Green	3	25
3. A Light in the Dark	3	25
4. Don Burns	3	25
5. New York	3	25

Answers to Pretest 2

PRETEST 2:   Page 1

Answers	Where Introduced	
	Unit	Lesson
1. fiction	4	37
2. author's last name	4	37

PRETEST 2:   Page 1

Answers	Where Introduced	
	Unit	**Lesson**
3. easy books	4	37
4. story collection	4	37
5. a, an, the	4	39
6. nonfiction	4	42
7. numbers	4	42
8. reference	4	44
9. card catalog	4	46
10. guide cards	4	48

PRETEST 2:   Page 2

Answers	Where Introduced	
	Unit	**Lesson**
1. The Wind Blows Free	4	37
2. Ginger Pye	4	37
3. The Hundred Dresses	4	37
4. Blue Willow	4	37
5. Drag Strip	4	37

PRETEST 2:   Page 3

Answers	Where Introduced	
	Unit	**Lesson**
1. 636.16 Rob	4	43
2. 636.3 Bro	4	43
3. 636.9 Sil	4	43
4. 638 Ste	4	42
5. 655 Bar	4	42

PRETEST 2:   Page 4

Answers	Where Introduced	
	Unit	**Lesson**
1. Joe Howard	4	50
2. 629.2 Bur	4	50

PRETEST 2:   Page 4

Answers	Where Introduced Unit	Lesson
3. Sweetwater Press	4	50
4. Bill Burton	4	50
5. 206	4	50
6. Cars, cars, cars	4	50
7. 1984	4	50
8. kites/knight	4	48
9. king/Kipling	4	48
10. Kipling/kites	4	48

Answers to Pretest 3

If the class lacks mastery of specific items, reteach the material. See the pages below, which designate where the items were introduced.

PRETEST 3:   Page 1

Answers	Where Introduced Unit	Lesson
1. science and geography	5	54
2. pseudonym	5	55
3. an illustrator card	5	56
4. an annotation	5	56
5. subject analytic card	5	56
6. articles	5	58
7. index	5	59
8. author, subject, title	4	46
	5	54
9. nonfiction	5	57
10. fiction	5	57

PRETEST 3:   Page 2

| Answers | Where Introduced | |
	Unit	Lesson
1. true	5	55
2. true	5	55
3. true	5	55
4. true	5	58
5. true	5	58
6. false	5	58
7. false	5	58
8. true	5	58
9. true	5	58
10. false	5	58
11. historical fiction	5	61
12. historical nonfiction	5	61
13. science nonfiction	5	61
14. science fiction	5	61
15. B	5	58
16. B	5	58
17. B	5	58
18. H	5	58
19. M	5	58
20. W	5	58

PRETEST 3:   Page 3

| Answers | Where Introduced | |
	Unit	Lesson
1. Harper and Row	5	50
2. Sarah, Plain and Tall	5	50
3. Patricia MacLachlan	5	50
4. 58	5	50
5. MacLachlan	5	50
6. 1985	5	50
7. fiction	5	50
8. It doesn't have a number.	5	50
9. no	5	50
10. Mac	5	50

APPENDIX C
WORKSHEET ANSWERS

UNIT 3

WORKSHEET 3.3: The Title Page

1. Ray Black
2. The New Girl
3. Janet Clark
4. New York
5. New Books

WORKSHEET 3.5: The Title Page

1. Jane Dickson
2. Animals You Know
3. Children's Books
4. Jane Dickson
5. San Francisco
6. c
7. d
8. a
9. b
10. e

WORKSHEET 3.10: The Title Page

1. Nan Hall
2. Frank Walker
3. Swinging on a Star
4. Bluebird Press
5. New York
6. title page
7. back
8. pictures

WORKSHEET 3.11: The Title Page

1. b
2. c
3. a

4. e
5. f
6. g
7. d

All About Fish
Bill Parker
Candy Miller
Dawson Company
England

WORKSHEET 3.14: The Table of Contents

1. The New Skates
2. 27
3. 35
4. 6
5. no
6. front

WORKSHEET 3.17: The Table of Contents

1. A Dog for Joe
2. 24
3. Ed Maxwell
4. 14
5. poems
6. The Boy Who Wasn't Afraid

WORKSHEET 3.23: The Index

1. 83–88
2. 84, 85, 87–89
3. 99–110
4. 100–101
5. 96, 108
6. 107
7. 109
8. schools

9. 18
10. 54–55

UNIT 4

WORKSHEET 4.2: Arranging Fiction Books

1. Brink
2. McCloskey
3. Robertson
4. Tobias
5. Williams

WORKSHEET 4.3: Arranging Fiction Books

Superfudge	Blume
Rufus M.	Estes
Ben and Me	Lawson
Winter Danger	Steele
Star Wars	Weinberg

WORKSHEET 4.4: Arranging Easy Books

Petunia	Duvoisin
Danny and the Dinosaur	Hoff
When I Was Young in the Mountains	Rylant
Sylvester and the Magic Pebble	Steig
Tale of a Black Cat	Withers

WORKSHEET 4.5: Arranging Fiction Books

Paddington Bear	Bond
Dear Mr. Henshaw	Cleary
Henry and Ribsy	Cleary
Ben and Me	Lawson
Mr. Revere and I	Lawson

WORKSHEET 4.6: Arranging Easy Books

Back Home	Brown
An Eagle Returns	Brown
The Story About Ping	Flack
Ox-Cart Man	Hall
Owl at Home	Lobel

WORKSHEET 4.7: Fiction Quiz

1. not true
2. the author's last name
3. Janet Gray
4. title
5. a, an, the

WORKSHEET 4.8: Arranging Fiction Books

Going Home	Bond
A Smile for Me	Bond
The New Car	Green
Lost in the Woods	Long
Ride the Wind	Turner

WORKSHEET 4.9: Arranging Nonfiction Books

1. true
2. number

    100
    200
    300
    400
    600
    700
    900

WORKSHEET 4.10: Arranging Nonfiction Books

    124
    398
    423
    507

636
745
973
220   B
323   T
410   L
510   M
629   C
770   N
800   A

WORKSHEET 4.11: Arranging Nonfiction Books

Set 1   Set 2
000   293
100   498
600   623
800   716
900   918

Set 3   Set 4
310   M   811
525   P   811.2
641   C   812
811   A
929   B

Set 5
917
917.20
917.8

Set 6
796
796.23
796.3

Set 7
636 B
636.14 C
636.3   A

WORKSHEET 4.12: Arranging Nonfiction Books

1. 599.4   Pye
2. 636.1   Cha

3. 636.8   Roc
4. 745.5   Lau
5. 979.8   Ada

WORKSHEET 4.13: Nonfiction Quiz

1. a
2. b
3. nonfiction
4. fiction
5. reference
6. reference
7. false
8. true
9. true
10. true

WORKSHEET 4.14: The Card Catalog

1. D
2. G
3. E–F
4. B
5. L
6. I–K
7. G
8. C
9. I–K
10. E–F

WORKSHEET 4.15: The Card Catalog

1. Q–S
2. Q–S
3. Q–S
4. W–Z
5. C–E
6. T–V
7. T–V
8. N–P
9. W–Z
10. I–K

WORKSHEET 4.16: Guide Cards

1. Animals–Art
2. America–Animals
3. America–Animals
4. A–Africa
5. A–Africa
6. Animals–Art
7. Art–Automobiles
8. Art–Automobiles
9. A–Africa
10. Africa–America

WORKSHEET 4.17: Guide Cards

1. B–Baseball
2. Boys–Browsing
3. Bell–Birds
4. B–Baseball
5. Birds–Boys
6. Baseball–Bell
7. Baseball–Bell
8. Boys–Browsing
9. Boys–Browsing
10. Bell–Birds

WORKSHEET 4.18: Guide Cards

1. R–Railroads
2. Rivers–Rome
3. Rivers–Rome
4. Reptiles–Rivers
5. Rome–
6. Reptiles–Rivers
7. Railroads–Reptiles
8. Railroads–Reptiles
9. Reptiles–Rivers
10. R–Railroads

WORKSHEET 4.19: Guide Cards

1. O–One-act Plays
2. O–One-act Plays
3. P–Perry
4. Perry–Plants
5. One-act Plays–P

6. Plants–Presidents
7. Plants–Presidents
8. Presidents–
9. P–Perry
10. Presidents–

WORKSHEET 4.22: The Card Catalog

1. The sign of the beaver
2. Elizabeth George Speare
3. Spe
4. Houghton Mifflin
5. 135
6. 1983
7. Speare
8. fiction
9. no number *or* author's letters
10. no

WORKSHEET 4.24: The Card Catalog

1. 1940
2. Macmillan
3. Call it courage
4. Spe
5. illustrations *or* pictures
6. Armstrong Sperry
7. 95
8. fiction
9. Sperry
10. Armstrong Sperry

UNIT 5

WORKSHEET 5.2: The Card Catalog

1. It's like this, Cat
2. Emily Neville
3. illustrations *or* pictures
4. 1963
5. Harper
6. Emil Weiss

7. 180
8. Nev
9. fiction
10. Neville

WORKSHEET 5.3: The Card Catalog

1. A Cowboys and cattle drives
   B Little house on the prairie
   C Spiders
2. A McCall
   B Wilder
   C Riedman
3. A 978 McC
   B Fic Wil
   C 595.44 Rie
4. A Childrens Press
   B Harper
   C Watts
5. A Carol Rogers
   B Garth Williams
   C (none listed)
6. A 127
   B 334
   C 48
7. A 1964
   B 1953
   C 1979
8. A subject
   B title
   C author

WORKSHEET 5.5: The Card Catalog

Each student will have a different answer. If possible, when a student hands his or her paper to you, grade and discuss it on the spot.

WORKSHEET 5.13: Encyclopedias

1. true
2. true
3. true
4. true
5. true
6. false
7. true
8. true
9. false
10. true
11. M
12. Y
13. J
14. R
15. R

WORKSHEET 5.14: Encyclopedias

1. Daniel Boone was the most famous pioneer of colonial times. (1734–1820)
2. U.S. and Canada
3. Eureka (I have found it.)
4. Zimbabwe, formerly called Rhodesia, is a landlocked country in southern Africa.
5. 1841
6. Any three of these answers: home, fortress, prison, armory, treasure house and center
7. An American aviator, who made the first solo flight across the Atlantic Ocean
8. English, French
9. 984 feet from the base
10. On the island of Komodo and on other small islands of Indonesia

UNIT 6

WORKSHEET 6.3: The Dewey Decimal System of Classification

1. 700
2. 800
3. 300

4. 500
5. 900
6. 400
7. 200
8. 000
9. 600
10. 100

WORKSHEET 6.4: The Card Catalog

1. h
2. f
3. d
4. a
5. g
6. b
7. c
8. e
9. author, title, subject
10. subject
11. a, an, the
12. It's in capitals.
13. first, alphabetically by country and subject (history) and second, chronologically by historical period
14. nonfiction
15. a person who draws (creates) the pictures for a book

WORKSHEET 6.5: The Card Catalog

1.	subject	L–M
2.	title	R
3.	author	E–F
4.	title	V–Z
5.	subject	L–M
6.	title	T–U
7.	subject	L–M
8.	author	E–F
9.	author	G
10.	title	T–U

WORKSHEET 6.6: The Card Catalog

1.	author	B
2.	title	E–F
3.	subject	L–M
4.	title	V–Z
5.	subject	C
6.	author	O–Q
7.	title	L–M
8.	author	C
9.	title	O–Q
10.	subject	I–K

WORKSHEET 6.7: The Card Catalog: Catalog Card Arrangement

Set 1	2	Set 2	3
	1		5
	3		1
	4		6
	5		2
			4
			7
Set 3	2	Set 4	2
	4		1
	3		3
	1		
	5		

WORKSHEET 6.9: Card Catalog Practice

This assignment is for classes using Worksheet 6.8 instead of a card catalog. Instructions for grading papers for classes using a card catalog are in Lesson 66.

Author Card

Author: *George, Jean Craighead*
Title: *My side of the mountain*
Illustrator: *Jean George*
Publisher: *Dutton*

Copyright date: *1959*
Number of pages: *178*
Call number: *Geo*

Title Card

Title: *Betty Crocker's cookbook for
    boys and girls*
Author: *Crocker, Betty*
Illustrator: *none listed*
Publisher: *Golden Press*
Copyright date: *1984*
Number of pages: *94*
Call number: *641.5 Cro*

Subject Card

Subject: *BASEBALL CARDS/
    baseball cards*
Author: *Clark, Steve*
Title: *The complete book of
    baseball cards*
Illustrator: *none listed*
Publisher: *Grosset and Dunlap*
Copyright date: *1976*
Number of pages: *112*
Call number: *769.5 Cla*

WORKSHEET 6.10: Biography and Autobiography

One, two, or three letters after the class number would be correct.

1. 920 Sur
2. 921 Lin
3. 920 Deu
4. 921 Hou
5. 920 Ler
6. 921 Bly
7. 920 Coy
8. 921 Car
9. 920 Hol
10. 920 Dav

APPENDIX D
BOOKS TO READ ALOUD

These books are graded as a general guide. Students and schools differ. Go above or below the grading if the book is appropriate for your students. Remember, every child is not going to be enthralled with every book. Before reading a book aloud to your students, read it through to yourself. A book designated for a particular holiday may not be specifically for that holiday, but the subject matter would be appropriate at that time. Refer to Appendix J, "Award-Winning Books" for more ideas.

General Titles

Title	Author	K	1	2	3	4	5	6	Holiday or Special Occasion
Alexander and the Terrible, Horrible, No Good, Very Bad Day	Judith Viorst		X	X	X				
Alexander, Who Used to Be Rich Last Sunday	Judith Viorst			X	X				
Amelia Bedelia	Peggy Parish		X	X	X				
The Aminal	Lorna Balian	X	X						
And to Think That I Saw It on Mulberry Street	Dr. Seuss		X	X	X				
Are You My Mother?	P. D. Eastman	X	X						
Ask Mr. Bear	Marjorie Flack	X	X						
Ben and Me	Robert Lawson						X	X	
Benjamin's 365 Birthdays	Judi Barrett	X	X						Birthday
Biggest Bear	Lynd Ward			X	X				
Black Stallion	Walter Farley			X	X	X	X	X	
Book of Giant Stories	David L. Harrison		X	X	X				
Boy Who Cried Wolf		X	X	X	X				
Boy Who Would Not Say His Name	Elizabeth Vreeken	X	X						

Title	Author	K	1	2	3	4	5	6	Holiday or Special Occasion
Bremen Town Musicians			X	X	X				
Brown Bear, Brown Bear, What Do You See? (Student participation)	Bill Martin, Jr.	X	X						
Caddie Woodlawn	Carol Ryrie Brink					X	X	X	
Cat in the Hat	Dr. Seuss		X	X	X				
A Chair for My Mother	Vera Williams				X	X			
Charlotte's Web	E. B. White					X	X	X	
Chicken Little		X	X						
Christmas Is a Time of Giving	Joan Walsh Anglund	X	X	X					Christmas
The Christmas Tree Forest	Raymond M. Alden					X	X	X	Christmas
Cinderella				X	X				
Clifford's Good Deeds and other Clifford books	Norman Bridwell	X	X	X					
Cloudy with a Chance of Meatballs	Judi Barrett	X	X	X	X				
Crictor	Toni Ungerer		X	X	X				
Cross-Country Cat	Mary Calhoun		X	X	X				
Crow Boy	Taro Yashima		X	X	X				
The Day Jimmy's Boa Ate the Wash	Trinka H. Noble	X	X	X					
Dick Whittington and His Cat	Marcia Brown		X	X	X				
Dragon and the Mouse	Stephen A. Timm	X	X	X					
Dragon and the Mouse: The Dream	Stephen A. Timm	X	X	X					
Dragon and the Mouse: Together Again	Stephen A. Timm	X	X	X					
Emperor's New Clothes			X	X	X				
Fat Cat	Jack Kent		X	X					
Five Chinese Brothers	Claire Bishop		X	X	X				

Title	Author								Notes
500 Hats of Bartholomew Cubbins	Dr. Seuss				X				
Frank Baber's Mother Goose Nursery Rhymes	Frank Baber		X	X					
Frog and Toad Are Friends	Arnold Lobel		X	X	X				
Frog and Toad Together	Arnold Lobel		X	X	X				
The Frog Prince	Paul Galdone				X	X			
Funny Thing	Wanda Gag		X	X					
Ghost Said Boo	John McInnes			X					Halloween
Gilberto and the Wind	Marie Hall Ets		X	X					
Gingerbread Boy	Paul Galdone		X	X	X				
Girl Who Loved Wild Horses	Paul Goble			X	X	X	X	X	Arbor Day
The Giving Tree	Shel Silverstein		X	X	X		X		
The Gnome from Nome and other Serendipity books	Stephen Cosgrove				X	X			
Golden Egg Book	Margaret Wise Brown		X	X					Easter
Golden Goose			X	X	X				
Goldilocks and the Three Bears			X	X	X				
Goodnight Moon	Margaret Wise Brown		X						
Green Eggs and Ham	Dr. Seuss		X	X	X				
Grouchy Ladybug	Eric Carle		X	X	X				
Gunniwolf (Student participation book)	Wilhelmina Harper		X	X	X				
Hamilton Duck	Arthur Getz		X	X					
Hamilton Duck's Springtime Story	Arthur Getz		X	X					Spring
Happy Prince	Oscar Wilde				X	X	X	X	
Hare and the Tortoise	Paul Galdone, illus.		X	X	X		X		
Harry and the Lady Next Door	Gene Zion		X	X	X				
Harry and the Terrible Whatzit	Dick Gackenbach		X	X	X				

Title	Author	K	1	2	3	4	5	6	Holiday or Special Occasion
Harry by the Sea	Gene Zion	X	X	X					
Harry the Dirty Dog	Gene Zion	X	X	X					
Henny Penny	Paul Galdone, illus.	X	X						
Henrietta, Circus Star	Syd Hoff	X	X	X					
Henry Explores the Jungle	Mark Taylor		X	X					
Henry Reed, Inc.	Keith Robertson					X	X	X	
Henry the Explorer	Mark Taylor	X	X						
Hidden Places	Phyllis Root				X	X	X	X	
Hole in the Dike	Norma B. Green			X	X				
Home for a Bunny	Margaret Wise Brown	X	X						Easter
Homer Price	Robert McCloskey					X	X	X	
Hot Air Henry	Mary Calhoun		X	X	X				
Humbug Rabbit	Lorna Balian	X	X	X	X				Easter
Humbug Witch	Lorna Balian	X	X	X					Halloween
Hundred Dresses	Eleanor Estes			X	X				
I Know an Old Lady	Rose Bonne	X	X	X	X				
I Want to Be a Bird	Joanne Kaiser	X							
If I Had a Dog	Lilian Obligado		X	X					
I'll Fix Anthony	Judith Viorst	X	X	X					
It Didn't Frighten Me	Janet L. Goss and Jerome C. Harste	X							Halloween
It's Like This, Cat	Emily Neville						X	X	
Jack and the Beanstalk	Art Seiden, illus.	X	X	X					
Jamie's Turn (Publish-A-Book winner)	Jamie De Witt, age 13				X	X	X	X	
Jane, Wishing (Story starter)	Tobi Tobias				X	X			

								Arbor Day
Johnny Appleseed (Match version to age)		X	X	X	X	X	X	Arbor Day
Just for You	Mercer Mayer	X	X	X				
Just Me and My Dad	Mercer Mayer	X	X	X	X			
Keep Your Mouth Closed, Dear	Aliki		X	X				
King Midas and the Golden Touch	Al Perkins	X	X	X				
Knock-Knock! Who's There?	Joseph Rosenbloom				X	X	X	
Knockout Knock Knocks	Caroline A. Levine			X	X	X	X	
Lassie Come-Home	Eric Knight				X	X	X	
Lazy Jack		X	X	X				
Lentil	Robert McCloskey	X	X	X	X			
Little Bear (For first story, dress a teddy bear as you tell the story.)	Else H. Minarik	X	X					
Little Black Sambo (Good for flannel board)	Helen Bannerman	X	X					
Little Old Man Who Could Not Read	Irma S. Black	X	X	X				Reading
Little Red Hen	Paul Galdone, illus.	X	X	X				
Little Red Riding Hood		X	X	X	X			
Loudest Noise in the World	Benjamin Elkin	X	X	X				Quietness
Madeline	Ludwig Bemelmans	X	X	X				
Madeline's Rescue	Ludwig Bemelmans	X	X	X				
Magic Porridge Pot	Paul Galdone, illus.		X	X				
Matchlock Gun	Walter Edmonds				X	X	X	
May I Bring a Friend?	Beatrice de Regniers	X	X	X				
Me and Caleb	Franklyn Mayer				X	X	X	
Merry Christmas Mom and Dad	Mercer Mayer	X	X	X				Christmas
Millions of Cats	Wanda Gag	X	X	X				
Ming Lo Moves the Mountain	Arnold Lobel	X	X	X				

Title	Author	K	1	2	3	4	5	6	Holiday or Special Occasion
Miss Nelson Is Missing	Harry Allard		X	X	X				
Miss Rumphius (Adapt to: How can you make the world a better place?)	Barbara Cooney			X	X				
Mr. Popper's Penguins	Richard and Florence Atwater					X	X	X	
The Mitten (Adapt to Christmas story)	Alvin Tresselt		X	X	X				Christmas
Momotaro	Mollie Clark, retold by		X	X	X				
A Monster Is Coming! A Monster Is Coming!	Florence Heide		X	X	X				
Mountain Boy (Publish-A-Book winner)	Anna Josephs, age 9				X	X	X	X	
Mouse Tales	Arnold Lobel			X	X				
Night in the Country	Cynthia Rylant		X	X	X				
Nine Days to Christmas	Marie Hall Ets			X	X	X			Christmas
No Roses for Harry	Gene Zion		X	X	X				
North to Freedom (Unforgettable book)	Anne Holm					X	X	X	
Old Woman and Her Pig	Paul Galdone, illus.		X	X	X				
Old Woman Who Swallowed a Fly			X	X	X				
On to Oregon	Honore Morrow							X	
One Good Deed Deserves Another	Katherine Evans		X	X	X				
Owl at Home	Arnold Lobel		X	X	X				
Ox-Cart Man	Donald Hall				X	X	X		
Pecos Bill and the Mustang	Harold W. Felton				X	X			
Pedro, the Angel of Olvera Street	Leo Politi				X	X			Christmas
Peter Rabbit	Beatrix Potter	X	X	X					Easter
Petunia	Roger Duvoisin		X	X	X				Books

Title	Author							
Pied Piper of Hamelin				X		X		
Pinocchio (Match version to age)	Carlo Collodi		X	X	X	X	X	
Play with Me	Marie Hall Ets	X	X					
Prince Bertram the Bad	Arnold Lobel	X	X	X				
Princess and the Pea			X	X				
Puss in Boots	Paul Galdone, illus.		X	X				
Quiet! There's a Canary in the Library	Don Freeman	X	X	X				Library
Rainbow of My Own	Don Freeman	X	X					Rainbow
Ramona the Pest	Beverly Cleary		X	X				
Rapunzel	the Brothers Grimm		X	X				
Rufus M.	Eleanor Estes		X	X				Library
Rumpelstiltskin	Paul Galdone, illus.	X	X	X				
Runaway Bunny	Margaret Wise Brown	X	X					Easter
Self-Control	Henrietta Gambill	X	X	X				Self-control
Shoemaker and the Elves		X	X	X				
Sleeping Beauty (Match version to age)			X	X	X	X	X	
Snow White and Rose Red	the Brothers Grimm		X	X				
Snow White and the Seven Dwarfs			X	X				
Something for Christmas	Palmer Brown		X	X				Christmas
Spooky Night	Natalie Carlson	X	X	X				Halloween
Stonecutter	Gerald McDermott		X	X				
Story About Ping	Marjorie Flack		X	X				
Strange Story of the Frog Who Became a Prince	Elinor Lander Horwitz			X	X	X		
Strega Nona	Tomie de Paola		X	X				
Stupids Step Out (and other Stupids books)	Harry Allard		X	X				

Title	Author	K	1	2	3	4	5	6	Holiday or Special Occasion
Sylvester and the Magic Pebble	William Steig		X	X	X				
Tale of a Black Cat (Chalkboard story)	Carl Withers	X	X						
There's No Such Thing as a Dragon	Jack Kent		X	X					
Three Bedtime Stories	Garth Williams, illus.	X	X						
Three Billy Goats Gruff		X	X	X					
Three Little Kittens		X	X						
Three Little Pigs		X	X						
Three Sillies	Paul Galdone, illus.	X	X	X	X				
Three Wishes		X	X	X	X				
Tikki Tikki Tembo	Arlene Mosel		X	X	X				
Tom Thumb		X	X	X	X				
Town Mouse and the Country Mouse	Paul Galdone, illus.		X	X	X				
A Tree Is Nice	Janice Udry	X	X	X	X				Arbor Day
Turtle and the Monkey: A Philippine Tale	Paul Galdone, illus.		X	X					
Turtle Tale	Frank Asch	X	X						
Ugly Duckling			X	X	X				
When I Was Young in the Mountains	Cynthia Rylant			X	X				
Where the Red Fern Grows	Wilson Rawls						X	X	
Where the Wild Things Are	Maurice Sendak	X	X						
Winter Danger	William Steele					X	X	X	
Wizard of Oz (Match version to age)	L. Frank Baum		X	X	X	X	X	X	
Woggle of Witches	Adrienne Adams	X	X	X					Halloween
Wolf and the Seven Kids		X	X	X					
You Never Can Tell	Janice Holland, adapter				X	X			

About Books and Libraries

Title	Author	Grade						
		K	1	2	3	4	5	6
Adventures of Cap'n O. G. Readmore The adventures of a cat who can't stay away from books and libraries. Scholastic paperback	Fran Manushkin, adapter	X	X	X				
Little Old Man Who Could Not Read An appealing and effective way to stress the importance of reading.	Irma Simonton Black			X	X			
Petunia A silly goose thinks that carrying a book will make her wise.	Roger Duvoisin		X	X	X			
Quiet! There's a Canary in the Library An appealing book which can be used to initiate a discussion of quietness in libraries.	Don Freeman	X	X	X	X			
Rufus M. Chapter 1 is a delightful account of how Rufus got a library card.	Eleanor Estes			X	X			
She Wanted to Read: The Story of Mary McLeod Bethune An inspiring, true story of a black girl who was determined to learn to read.	Ella Kaiser Carruth				X	X	X	X

POETRY

Miscellaneous Categories

Title	Author	K	1	2	3	4	5	6
Barbara Frietchie	John Greenleaf Whittier					X	X	X
Book of Americans	Rosemary and Stephen Benet				X	X	X	X
Casey at the Bat	Ernest Thayer				X	X	X	X
Everybody Needs a Rock	Byrd Baylor			X	X	X		
The Gobble-Uns 'll Git You Ef You Don't Watch Out! (Read for Halloween)	James Whitcomb Riley		X	X	X			
Hailstones and Halibut Bones	Mary O'Neill		X	X	X	X	X	X
Hiawatha (Illustrated by Susan Jeffers)	Henry Wadsworth Longfellow				X	X	X	X
In a Pumpkin Shell	Joan Walsh Anglund	X	X					
Stopping by Woods on a Snowy Evening (exquisite illustrations by Susan Jeffers)	Robert Frost				X	X	X	X
Where the Sidewalk Ends	Shel Silverstein		X	X	X	X	X	X

BOOKS FOR HISPANIC STUDENTS

Title	Author						
. . . And Now Miguel	Joseph Krumgold					X	X
Are You My Mother? (in Spanish and English)	P. D. Eastman	X	X				
Gilberto and the Wind	Marie Hall Ets	X	X	X			
Little Red Hen: La Pequena Gallina Roja	Letty Williams	X	X	X	X		
Nine Days to Christmas	Marie Hall Ets		X	X	X	X	
One Good Deed Deserves Another	Katherine Evans		X	X	X		
Pedro, the Angel of Olvera Street	Leo Politi			X	X	X	
Piggy Bank Gonzales	Jack Kent		X	X			
When the Monkeys Wore Sombreros	Mariana Beeching de Prieto		X	X	X		

MISCELLANEOUS TITLES

Title	Author			
First Grade Jitters (First grade teachers, read on the first day of school.)	Robert Quackenbush		X	
Giants and Other Plays for Kids	Syd Hoff	X	X	X
Hill of Fire (easy nonfiction for student reading—Mexican background)	Thomas P. Lewis	X	X	X

Paperback Titles

Title	Author	Publisher/I.D.	K	1	2	3	4	5	6
Bow Wow! Meow! A First Book of Sounds	Melanie Bellah	A Little Golden Book	X						
Eloise Wilkin's Mother Goose	Eloise Wilkin	A Little Golden Book	X	X					
Montgomery Moose's Favorite Riddles	Mike Thaler	Scholastic				X	X	X	X
My Home	Renee Bartkowski	A Little Golden Book	X	X					
Old Mother Hubbard	Aurelius Battaglia, illus.	A Little Golden Book	X	X					
Raggedy Ann and Andy Book (Tells all the things a friend is.)	Jean Sukus	A Golden Shape Book	X	X					
Rapunzel (Beautifully illustrated. Read the story aloud and then let the students read it.)	Bernice Chardiet	Scholastic			X				
(Serendipity Books)	Stephen Cosgrove	Price/Stern and Sloan				X	X		
Someone Is Eating the Sun (Amusing story which introduces the eclipse.)	Ruth A. Sonneborn Eric Gurney, illus.	Random House Pictureback	X	X	X				
Who Are You?	Joan and Roger Bradfield	Whitman	X	X	X				

APPENDIX E
ILLUSTRATIONS TO SHARE

You may want to use these books in one of two ways. One, select a book from the list. Read it, share the pictures, and discuss their artistic appeal. Two, show the pictures from several books, discuss their artistic appeal, and then invite the students to examine the books at a specified time during the day.

Teachers of kindergarten through third grade: National Geographic's Books for Young Explorers feature excellent photographs. If your library doesn't have any of these high-interest books, buy a set for your room. A set of four books sells for approximately $12. Examples of the titles found in a set are *What Happens at the Zoo, Exploring the Seashore, Baby Farm Animals,* and *The Wonderful World of Seals and Whales.*

When teaching about illustrations, include some outstanding photographs.

Because art is ageless, these books are graded by their read-aloud levels.

Title	Author	Illustrator	K	1	2	3	4	5	6
America's Ethan Allen	Stewart Holbrook	Lynd Ward					X	X	X
Animal Friends and Neighbors	Jan Pfloog	Jan Pfloog	X	X	X				
Big Hungry Bear	Don Wood and Audrey Wood	Don Wood	X	X					
Biggest Bear	Lynd Ward	Lynd Ward			X	X			
Black Horse	Marianna Mayer	Katie Thamer				X	X	X	X
Circus Is Coming	Hilary Knight	Hilary Knight	X		X				
Crictor	Tomi Ungerer	Tomi Ungerer	X	X	X	X			
Crow Boy	Taro Yashima	Taro Yashima	X	X	X	X			
A Friend Is Someone Who Likes You	Joan Walsh Anglund	Joan Walsh Anglund	X	X	X				
Gift of the Sacred Dog	Paul Goble	Paul Goble				X	X	X	X
Girl Who Loved Wild Horses	Paul Goble	Paul Goble				X	X	X	X
Giving Tree	Shel Silverstein	Shel Silverstein	X	X	X	X			
Golden Egg Book	Margaret Wise Brown	Leonard Weisgard	X	X					
Hiawatha	Henry Wadsworth Longfellow	Susan Jeffers				X	X	X	X

Title	Author	Illustrator	K	1	2	3	4	5	6
									Grade
Hide-and-Seek Duck	Cyndy Szekeres	Cyndy Szekeres	X						
Home for a Bunny	Margaret Wise Brown	Garth Williams	X	X					
Humbug Rabbit	Lorna Balian	Lorna Balian	X	X	X	X			
In a Pumpkin Shell	Joan Walsh Anglund	Joan Walsh Anglund	X	X					
Jack and the Beanstalk		Art Seiden	X	X	X				
Jamie's Turn	Jamie De Witt, age 13	Julie Brinckloe				X	X	X	X
Madeline's Rescue	Ludwig Bemelmans	Ludwig Bemelmans	X	X	X	X			
Miss Rumphius	Barbara Cooney	Barbara Cooney			X	X			
Mountain Boy	Anna Josephs, age 9	Bill Ersland				X	X	X	X
Night in the Country	Cynthia Rylant	Mary Szilagyi		X	X	X			
Ox-Cart Man	Donald Hall	Barbara Cooney	X		X	X	X	X	
Peter Rabbit	Beatrix Potter	Beatrix Potter	X	X	X				
Rain (wordless)	Peter Spier	Peter Spier	X	X	X	X			
Quick as a Cricket	Audrey Wood	Don Wood	X	X					
Someone Is Eating the Sun Random House Pictureback	Ruth A. Sonneborn	Eric Gurney		X	X				
Star Boy	Paul Goble	Paul Goble				X	X	X	X
Stopping by Woods on a Snowy Evening	Robert Frost	Susan Jeffers				X	X	X	X
Sylvester and the Magic Pebble	William Steig	William Steig		X	X	X			
Three Bedtime Stories	Garth Williams, retold by	Garth Williams	X	X					
Thumbelina	Hans Christian Anderson	Susan Jeffers			X	X			
A Tree Is Nice	Janice Udry	Marc Simont	X	X	X	X			
Unicorn and the Lake	Marianna Mayer	Michael Hague				X	X		
Where the Wild Things Are	Maurice Sendak	Maurice Sendak	X	X					
Wild Animals and Their Babies	Jan Pfloog	Jan Pfloog	X	X	X	X			

APPENDIX F
ILLUSTRATORS' STYLES AND CHARACTERISTICS

Illustrator	Styles/Characteristics
Anglund, Joan Walsh	Charm, quaintness, diminutive format
Bemelmans, Ludwig	*Madeline's Rescue*, the 1954 Caldecott medal winner, expresses action, wild exaggeration, humor
Brown, Marcia	Has several styles *Dick Whittington and His Cat*—brown and black linoleum cuts, vigorous, full of movement, bold
Ets, Marie Hall	*Play with Me*—subtle and exquisite pastel illustrations
Galdone, Paul	Humor, shows emotions in facial expressions
Goble, Paul	*The Girl Who Loved Wild Horses*, the 1979 Caldecott winner, is a book of exquisite, stylized illustrations. *Star Boy*—ALA Booklist says, "Goble uses intense, pure colors that add vibrancy to his delicate designs. His style combines simple geometric forms, stylized Indian motifs, and lacy details of landscape and apparel into masterfully coordinated spreads that are a visual delight. A considered, reverent, and eye-catching rendition of an important native American legend." (Reprinted with permission of the American Library Association.)
Hoff, Syd	Cartooning style
Keats, Ezra Jack	*Snowy Day*, the 1963 Caldecott winner, conveys freedom and freshness. The little boy expresses action and life.
Lawson, Robert	Humor, tenderness, appealing subjects
Lionni, Leo	Deals with objects in nature, animals; never realistic Reactions of animals are those of human beings Uses mixed media: collage and water color with pencil or charcoal *Swimmy* and *Frederick*—torn paper, mixed media
McCloskey, Robert	Humorous realism
Potter, Beatrix	Got her inspiration from the natural world, drawings and water colors
Schulz, Charles	Cartooning style

Illustrator	Styles/Characteristics
Sendak, Maurice	*Where the Wild Things Are*, the 1964 Caldecott winner, expresses great originality. Its preposterous animals are delightful.
Seuss, Dr.	Zany humor, outlandish animals
Silverstein, Shel	Line drawings
Simont, Marc	*A Tree Is Nice*, the 1957 Caldecott winner, expresses warmth of color and feeling.
Spier, Peter	Expresses vitality, shows great detail
Steig, William	Humor, tenderness; generally uses watercolors *Sylvester and the Magic Pebble*, the 1970 Caldecott winner, is an example of how Steig humanizes animals with clothing and facial expressions.
Ward, Lynd	Uses shading to create mood and character in the 1953 Caldecott medal winner, *The Biggest Bear* *America's Ethan Allen*—Ward uses brilliant, unexpected colors to highlight and enhance his illustrations.
Williams, Garth	Personifies animals Often has full-color picture books

APPENDIX G
BOOKS FOR TEACHERS AND LIBRARIANS

Books Kids Will Sit Still For: A Guide to Using Children's Literature for Librarians, Teachers and Parents by Judy Freeman, Freline, 1984

Lists and annotates read-aloud books by grade level. Gives ideas for student participation and for celebrating books. Tells how to give book talks. Highly recommended.

The Read-Aloud Handbook by Jim Trelease, Penguin, 1985

Annotated, graded list of books to read aloud. Chapters on why to read aloud, when to begin to read aloud, and so forth.

Children's Literature from A to Z a guide for parents and teachers by Jon C. Stott, McGraw-Hill, 1984

Biographies of authors and illustrators are interfiled alphabetically with brief articles on ABC Books, Animal Stories, Biography, The Caldecott Medal, Cinderella, Fables, Fantasy, Myths, and so forth. The tips for parents and teachers are especially useful.

Children's Books Too Good to Miss by May Hill Arbuthnot and others, Press of Western Reserve University, 1966; revised and enlarged 1979

Graded, annotated books for young people through age fourteen by the distinguished author May Hill Arbuthnot. Includes a section entitled "The Artist and Children's Books," which discusses individual illustrators and their works.

How to Read and Write Poetry by Anna Cosman, Watts, 1979

The title of this book, *How to Read and Write Poetry,* describes its contents very succinctly. Although written for young people, teachers may find this approach to poetry one they can use.

Write Your Own Story by Vivian Dubrovin, Watts, 1984

This book tells how to write a short story. Although written for young people, it could be used as a teacher's lesson plan for teaching story writing.

APPENDIX H
ADDRESSES OF AUTHORS,
ILLUSTRATORS, AND PUBLISHERS

Write to the authors and illustrators in care of their publishers.

Authors and Illustrators

Aiken, Joan (Delacorte)
Anno, Mitsumasa (Putnam)
Aruego, Jose (Greenwillow)
Asimov, Isaac (Doubleday)
Berenstain, Jan and Stan (Random House)
Blume, Judy (Bradbury Press)
Brown, Marcia (Scribner)
Byars, Betsy (Delacorte)
Carle, Eric (Harper and Row)
Cleary, Beverly (Morrow)
Dahl, Roald (Knopf)
de Paola, Tomie (Putnam)
Emberley, Ed (Little, Brown)
Fleischman, Sid (Random House)
Fritz, Jean (Putnam)
George, Jean C. (Harper and Row)
Goble, Paul (Bradbury Press)
Haywood, Carolyn (Morrow)
Hoban, Lillian (Harper and Row)
Hoban, Russell (Harper and Row)
Konigsburg, E. L. (Macmillan)
Le Guin, Ursula K. (Macmillan)
L'Engle, Madeleine (Farrar, Straus
    and Giroux)
Lionni, Leo (Pantheon)
Lobel, Anita (Harper and Row)
Lobel, Arnold (Harper and Row)

Lowry, Lois (Houghton Mifflin)
McPhail, David (Dutton)
Marshall, James (Houghton Mifflin)
Mayer, Mercer (Western Pub.)
O'Dell, Scott (Houghton Mifflin)
Peet, Bill (Houghton Mifflin)
Prelutsky, Jack (Greenwillow)
Quackenbush, Robert (Prentice-Hall)
Scarry, Richard (Random House)
Schulz, Charles (Random House)
Sendak, Maurice (Harper and Row)
Seuss, Dr. (Random House)
Silverstein, Shel (Harper and Row)
Singer, Isaac Bashevis (Farrar, Straus
    and Giroux)
Sobol, Donald (Lodestar)
Steig, William (Farrar, Straus and
    Giroux)
Stevenson, James (Greenwillow)
Tudor, Tasha (McKay)
Viorst, Judith (Macmillan)
Wildsmith, Brian (Oxford University
    Press)
Zemach, Margot (Farrar, Straus and
    Giroux)
Zolotow, Charlotte (Harper and Row)

Publishers

Bradbury Press, Inc. (Affiliate of
    Macmillan, Inc.), 866 Third Ave., New
    York, NY 10022
Delacorte Press, 1 Dag Hammarskjold
    Plaza, 245 E. 47th St., New York, NY
    10017

Doubleday and Co., Inc. (Division of
    Bantam Doubleday Dell Publishing)
    666 Fifth Ave., New York, NY 10103
Dutton, E. P., Inc. (Division of NAL/
    Penguin), 2 Park Ave., New York, NY
    10016

Farrar, Straus and Giroux, Inc., 19 Union Square W., New York, NY 10003

Greenwillow Books (Division of William Morrow and Co., Inc.) 105 Madison Ave., New York, NY 10016

Harper and Row Publishers, Inc., 10 E. 53rd St., New York, NY 10022

Houghton Mifflin Company, 1 Beacon St., Boston, MA 02108

Knopf, Alfred A. (Subsidiary of Random House, Inc.), 201 E. 50th St., New York, NY 10022

Little, Brown and Company (Division of Time, Inc.), 34 Beacon St., Boston MA 02108

Lodestar Books, 2 Park Avenue, New York, NY 10016

Lothrop, Lee and Shepard Books (See Morrow)

McKay, David, Co., Inc. (Subsidiary of Random House, Inc.), 201 E. 50th St., New York, NY 10022

Macmillan Publishing Co., Inc., 866 Third Ave., New York, NY 10022

Morrow, William, and Co., Inc., 105 Madison Ave., New York, NY 10016

Oxford University Press, Inc., 200 Madison Ave., New York, NY 10016

Pantheon Books (Division of Random House, Inc.), 201 E. 50th St., New York, NY 10022

Prentice-Hall, Rte. 9W, Englewood Cliffs, NJ 07632

Putnam Publishing Group, 200 Madison Ave., New York, NY 10016

Random House, Inc., 201 E. 50th Street, New York, NY 10022

Scribner's, Charles, Sons, 866 Third Ave., New York, NY 10022

Western Publishing Co., Inc., 850 Third Ave., New York, NY 10022

Note

You can obtain the address of an author or illustrator by one of the methods below.

1. If you have access to a book by the author or illustrator, obtain the publisher's name from the title page. Refer to the list above for the publisher's address. If the publisher's address isn't listed, phone your local reference librarian and request it.

2. At you local public library, look under the author's name in the appropriate author volume of *Books in Print* to obtain the name of the author's publisher. Then look in the publisher volume of *Books in Print* for the publisher's address.

3. Phone your local library and ask for the reference librarian. Tell the librarian that you need to know who publishes the author's (illustrator's) books and you need to know the publisher's address.

APPENDIX I
PUBLISH-A-BOOK CONTEST

BASIC REQUIREMENTS

Contestants	Any fourth, fifth, or sixth grade U.S. or Canadian student
Theme	Folk tales, tall tales, and fairy tales
Literary type	Fiction or nonfiction
Number of words	700–800 (typed, double-spaced)
Grand prize	$500, a contract with royalties, publication of the winner's book, and 10 free copies Four grand prizes will be awarded The sponsor named on each of the grand prize entries will receive 20 free books from the Raintree catalog.
Honorable mention	20 honorable mention winners will receive $25 each The sponsor named on each of the honorable mention entries will receive 10 free books from the Raintree catalog
Deadline	Manuscripts must be postmarked by January 31, 1990
Sponsor	Raintree Publishers 310 West Wisconsin Avenue Milwaukee, Wisconsin 53203 Telephone 1-800-558-1580
Note	All prize money will be paid in U.S. dollars.

Other Requirements

1. The contestant must have a sponsor, either a teacher or a librarian.
2. All manuscripts must include the writer's name, address, phone number, grade, and age, and also the sponsor's name, address, and phone number.

SUGGESTIONS

1. You may want to read the four 1988 grand prize winning books to your students. They are:

    Huan Ching and the Golden Fish
    by Michael Reeser, sixth grade
    Gilmer, Texas

    The Luck of the Irish
    by Brendan Patrick Paulsen, sixth grade
    Silverdale, Washington

A Very Scraggly Christmas Tree
by Christie Pippen, sixth grade
Crossett, Arkansas

Only At the Children's Table
by Daria Baron-Hall, sixth grade
Port Allegany, Pennsylvania

2. If these books are not in your school or public library, ask your public library to obtain them for you through interlibrary loan.

3. Contact the sponsor each year to get information about the current contest.

APPENDIX J
AWARD-WINNING BOOKS

The Caldecott Medal

The Caldecott medal is an annual award given to the illustrator of the most distinguished picture book for children published during the preceding year. A list of Caldecott medal winners appears below.

Winners of the Caldecott Medal

Year	Illustrator	Winning Book	Year	Illustrator	Winning Book
1938	Dorothy P. Lathrop	Animals of the Bible	1966	Nonny Hogrogian	Always Room for One More
1939	Thomas Handforth	Mei Li	1967	Evaline Ness	Sam, Bangs, & Moonshine
1940	Ingri and Edgar Parin d'Aulaire	Abraham Lincoln	1968	Ed Emberley	Drummer Hoff
1941	Robert Lawson	They Were Strong and Good	1969	Uri Shulevitz	The Fool of the World and the Flying Ship
1942	Robert McCloskey	Make Way for Ducklings	1970	William Steig	Sylvester and the Magic Pebble
1943	Virginia Lee Burton	The Little House	1971	Gail E. Haley	A Story—A Story
1944	Louis Slobodkin	Many Moons	1972	Nonny Hogrogian	One Fine Day
1945	Elizabeth Orton Jones	Prayer for a Child	1973	Blair Lent	The Funny Little Woman
1946	Maud and Miska Petersham	The Rooster Crows	1974	Margot Zemach	Duffy and the Devil
1947	Leonard Weisgard	The Little Island	1975	Gerald McDermott	Arrow to the Sun: A Pueblo Indian Tale
1948	Roger Duvoisin	White Snow, Bright Snow	1976	Leo and Diane Dillon	Why Mosquitoes Buzz in People's Ears: A West African Tale
1949	Berta and Elmer Hader	The Big Snow	1977	Leo and Diane Dillon	Ashanti to Zulu: African Traditions
1950	Leo Politi	Songs of the Swallows	1978	Peter Spier	Noah's Ark
1951	Katherine Milhous	The Egg Tree	1979	Paul Goble	The Girl Who Loved Wild Horses
1952	Nicolas Mordvinoff	Finders Keepers	1980	Barbara Cooney	Ox-Cart Man
1953	Lynd K. Ward	The Biggest Bear	1981	Arnold Lobel	Fables
1954	Ludwig Bemelmans	Madeline's Rescue	1982	Chris Van Allsburg	Jumanji
1955	Marcia Brown	Cinderella; or The Little Glass Slipper	1983	Marcia Brown	Shadow
1956	Feodor Rojankovsky	Frog Went A-Courtin'	1984	Alice and Martin Provensen	The Glorious Flight: Across the Channel with Louis Bleriot
1957	Marc Simont	A Tree Is Nice	1985	Trina Schart Hyman	Saint George and the Dragon
1958	Robert McCloskey	Time of Wonder	1986	Chris Van Allsburg	The Polar Express
1959	Barbara Cooney	Chanticleer and the Fox	1987	Richard Egielski	Hey, Al
1960	Marie Hall Ets	Nine Days to Christmas	1988	Jane Yolen	Owl Moon
1961	Nicolas Sidjakov	Baboushka and the Three Kings	1989	Stephen Gammell	Song and Dance Man
1962	Marcia Brown	Once a Mouse			
1963	Ezra Jack Keats	The Snowy Day			
1964	Maurice Sendak	Where the Wild Things Are			
1965	Beni Montresor	May I Bring a Friend?			

The Newbery Medal

The Newbery medal is an annual award given to the author of the most distinguished American book for children published in the preceding year. A list of Newbery medal winners appears below.

Winners of the Newbery Medal

Year	Author	Winning Book	Year	Author	Winning Book
1922	Hendrik Van Loon	The Story of Mankind	1957	Virginia Sorensen	Miracles on Maple Hill
1923	Hugh Lofting	The Voyages of Dr. Dolittle	1958	Harold V. Keith	Rifles for Watie
1924	Charles Hawes	The Dark Frigate	1959	Elizabeth G. Speare	The Witch of Blackbird Pond
1925	Charles Finger	Tales from Silver Lands	1960	Joseph Krumgold	Onion John
1926	Arthur Chrisman	Shen of the Sea	1961	Scott O'Dell	Island of the Blue Dolphins
1927	Will James	Smoky	1962	Elizabeth G. Speare	The Bronze Bow
1928	Dhan Mukerji	Gay-Neck	1963	Madeleine L'Engle	A Wrinkle in Time
1929	Eric P. Kelly	The Trumpeter of Krakow	1964	Emily C. Neville	It's Like This, Cat
1930	Rachel Field	Hitty, Her First Hundred Years	1965	Maia Wojciechowska	Shadow of a Bull
1931	Elizabeth Coatsworth	The Cat Who Went to Heaven	1966	Elizabeth Borton de Treviño	I, Juan de Pareja
1932	Laura Armer	Waterless Mountain	1967	Irene Hunt	Up a Road Slowly
1933	Elizabeth Lewis	Young Fu of the Upper Yangtze	1968	Elaine Konigsburg	From the Mixed-Up Files of Mrs. Basil E. Frankweiler
1934	Cornelia Meigs	Invincible Louisa			
1935	Monica Shannon	Dobry	1969	Lloyd Alexander	The High King
1936	Carol Ryrie Brink	Caddie Woodlawn	1970	William H. Armstrong	Sounder
1937	Ruth Sawyer	Roller Skates	1971	Betsy Byars	The Summer of the Swans
1938	Kate Seredy	The White Stag	1972	Robert C. O'Brien	Mrs. Frisby and the Rats of NIMH
1939	Elizabeth Enright	Thimble Summer	1973	Jean C. George	Julie of the Wolves
1940	James Daugherty	Daniel Boone	1974	Paula Fox	The Slave Dancer
1941	Armstrong Sperry	Call It Courage	1975	Virginia Hamilton	M. C. Higgins, the Great
1942	Walter D. Edmonds	The Matchlock Gun	1976	Susan Cooper	The Grey King
1943	Elizabeth Janet Gray	Adam of the Road	1977	Mildred Taylor	Roll of Thunder, Hear My Cry
1944	Esther Forbes	Johnny Tremain	1978	Katherine Paterson	Bridge to Terabithia
1945	Robert Lawson	Rabbit Hill	1979	Ellen Raskin	The Westing Game
1946	Lois Lenski	Strawberry Girl	1980	Joan Blos	A Gathering of Days: A New England Girl's Journal
1947	Carolyn S. Bailey	Miss Hickory			
1948	William Pène du Bois	The Twenty-One Balloons	1981	Katherine Paterson	Jacob Have I Loved
1949	Marguerite Henry	King of the Wind	1982	Nancy Willard	A Visit to William Blake's Inn
1950	Marguerite de Angeli	The Door in the Wall	1983	Cynthia Voigt	Dicey's Song
1951	Elizabeth Yates	Amos Fortune, Free Man	1984	Beverly Cleary	Dear Mr. Henshaw
1952	Eleanor Estes	Ginger Pye	1985	Robin McKinley	The Hero and the Crown
1953	Ann Nolan Clark	Secret of the Andes	1986	Patricia MacLachlan	Sarah, Plain and Tall
1954	Joseph Krumgold	. . . And Now Miguel	1987	Sid Fleischman	The Whipping Boy
1955	Meindert DeJong	The Wheel on the School	1988	Russell Freedman	Lincoln: A Photo-Biography
1956	Jean Lee Latham	Carry On, Mr. Bowditch	1989	Paul Fleischman	Joyful Noise: Poems for Two Voices

Glossary

annotation: A description of a book's contents.

author: A person who writes a book or other literary work.

author card: A catalog card which has the author's name on the first line.

autobiography: A true story of one's life, written by oneself.

biography: A true story of a person's life, written by another person.

Caldecott medal: An annual award given to the illustrator of the most distinguished picture book for children during the preceding year.

call number: The Dewey Decimal Classification number and one, two, or three letters of the author's name, or in the case of biography, the biographee's name. Examples: 613 S, 613 Sm, 613 Smi. Biography: 921 W, 921 Wa, 921 Was.

card catalog: An index to the books in a library made on separate cards and filed alphabetically.

chapter: A main division of a book.

class number: A classification number, which represents a book's subject. Examples: 613, 921.

collective biography: A collection of biographies.

contents: Variant term for table of contents.

copyright: The exclusive right to publish, produce, or sell a book, play, or other literary work. A legal protection of literary rights.

cross reference: A "see" cross reference directs one to another heading. A "see also" cross reference refers one to where additional information about a subject can be found.

Dewey Decimal System of Classification: The classification system most generally used in libraries in which knowledge is divided into ten major groups by subject. Each group can be subdivided indefinitely by using decimals.

easy books: Easy-to-read fiction books.

edition: Copies of a book printed from the same plates and type and which are published at about the same time.

entry words: The listing, in an index, dictionary, encyclopedia, and so forth, of words that are the subject of consideration.

fiction: Books that are made up, untrue.

glossary: Definitions of special or difficult words in a book.

guide words: Words at the top of a page, or at the top of facing pages, that help you determine alphabetically whether the word you are looking for is found between them.

half title page: A page on which only a book's title appears. It precedes the title page.

hardback: A book bound in a stiff cover.

historical fiction: A book, or other literary work, that has an historical background or basis, but which is fiction.

historical nonfiction: A book, or other literary work, that is historically true.

illustration: A picture, design, or diagram used to explain or decorate a book, magazine, and so forth.

illustrator: A person who makes pictures, designs, or diagrams for a book, magazine, and so forth.

illustrator card: A catalog card that has the illustrator's name on the first line.

index: An alphabetical list of the main subjects in a book, including the page numbers on which they can be found.

librarian: A person trained in library science who works in a library.

library: A room or building where there are many books for reading.

National Children's Book Week: A week set aside each year in November to promote reading among young people.

Newbery medal: An annual award given to the author of the most distinguished American book for children published in the preceding year.

nonfiction: Books, or other literary works, that are true.

paperback: A book bound with a paper cover.

place of publication: Where a book is published.

publisher: A person or company that produces printed materials.

reference book: A nonfiction book which is not designed to be read from cover to cover, but to which one refers for quick information. Reference books can't be checked out of libraries. Expensive books are usually put in reference sections. Dictionaries and encyclopedias are reference books.

revised edition: Copies of a book that have been corrected, improved, or brought up-to-date.

science fiction: Literature that takes as its premise a scientific breakthrough or achievement and extrapolates from that projection into the future in logical sequence. Distinguished from fantasy in that science fiction operates within what might really be.

science nonfiction: Books, or other literary works, about science that are true.

spine: The strip that joins the front and back covers of a book.

spine ———→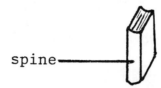

story collection: Books that contain a collection of stories.

subject analytic card: A catalog card which has the subject and pages of a part of a book on the top line.

subject card: A catalog card which has the subject of the book on the top line.

table of contents: A list of stories, chapters, or poems in a book, arranged in the order of their appearance.

title: The name of a book, poem, chapter, and so forth.

title card: A catalog card that has the title of the book on the top line.

title page: A page near the beginning of a book, on which the name of the author, title, illustrator, series (if any), publisher, and the place of publication appear.

tracing: A record of all the catalog cards made for a book. Printed at the bottom of catalog cards for the librarian's use.

volume: One of the books of a set; a single book complete in itself.

Index